CitizenJean

CitizenJean

RIOTS, ROGUES, RUMORS, AND OTHER INSIDE SEATTLE STORIES

JEAN GODDEN

WSU
PRESS

Washington State University Press
Pullman, Washington

WSU PRESS
WASHINGTON STATE UNIVERSITY

Washington State University Press
PO Box 645910
Pullman, Washington 99164-5910
Phone: 800-354-7360
Email: wsupress@wsu.edu
Website: wsupress.wsu.edu

Library of Congress Cataloging-in-Publication Data
Names: Godden, Jean H., author.
Title: Citizen Jean : riots, rogues, rumors, and other inside Seattle stories
    / Jean Godden.
Description: Pullman, Washington : Washington State University Press, 2019.
    | Includes bibliographical references and index.
Identifiers: LCCN 2018044852 | ISBN 9780874223637 (alk. paper)
Subjects: LCSH: Godden, Jean H. | Journalists--Washington
    (State)--Seattle--Biography. | Women journalists--Washington
    (State)--Seattle--Biography. | Women civic leaders--Washington
    (State)--Seattle--Biography.
Classification: LCC PN4874.G495 A3 2019 | DDC 070.92 [B] --dc23 LC record
available at https://lccn.loc.gov/2018044852

On the cover: Jean Godden at Pike Place Market.
Seattle Municipal Archives, Item 170589

Contents

Foreword

The only certainty is that Seattle is about to change. It has been changing from its founding as a pioneer settlement on the Northwest frontier in the nineteenth century. Today it continues to transform, to undergo conversion in both a territorial sense and its public image.

It's hard for historians to keep up with a city changing as fast as Seattle. And maybe that's why there have been so few histories of Seattle. Perhaps it's a job best suited for a journalist, someone used to breaking news and sudden deadlines. And not just any journalist—but one with a sharp eye, a quick wit, and an insatiable curiosity about the city that was, and the city that is about to be.

The truth is, we've been blessed to have that observer for more than fifty years. Jean Godden is an adopted daughter of the city. She came here with her much-traveled military family at the age of seventeen. She often speaks of that arrival and the realization she had, at last, found her roots.

Over the years, Godden has had rare opportunities to observe Seattle's changing scene. She watched the city, first as a reporter, then an editor, and finally as a city columnist at the *Seattle Post-Intelligencer* and later at the *Seattle Times*. Her beat was sometimes as narrow as the Pike Place Market and, more often, as broad as the city itself.

After two decades working as a columnist, she left the newspaper world and ran for public office. She won a seat on the Seattle City Council and served the city through twelve of its changing years. She saw Seattle go through the glory days of the Microsoft boom, hit a bad patch during the Great Recession, and then exploded with supercharged economic growth, as the city transformed into an Amazon-Starbucks-Costco-Microsoft-Medico-Industrial giant.

More than ever, the city's citizens are aware that the salt water that laps the pilings of the waterfront has opened the city to the oceans of the world. The mountains that surround and shelter the city have given it a framework and a springboard, a setting too grand to ever have been imagined. The constant rain, although deplored by some, provides the iridescent light that lends itself to dreams. Seattle dreams big.

Dreams realized are some of the stories that Jean imparts here. She recounts tales from Century 21, the world's fair that placed Seattle on the map; she tells how a determined group of citizens saved Seattle from those who would bury it forever under freeway lanes. She describes the yeasty 1970's newspaper culture, contentious years with the state's mercurial woman governor, the fight to save the Pike Place Public Market from New York investors, and the chaos that gripped the city during the World Trade Organization debacle.

Godden provides insights into the city's costly and disastrous newspaper strike and the long and bitter war between the city's rival newspapers. She reports on the city's struggles to survive its leanest days since the Great Depression and attempts at narrowing the nation's largest gender wage gap. Finally, she ends with insider's look at the stigma women face when running for office.

Godden tells these tales as only she can. Like a veteran reporter, she reveals the who, what, when, where, why, and how of changing Seattle and gives us insight into some of the stories she never told.

For years, those of us who love our city have taken special pleasure that Jean was there with us, notebook in hand, pencil poised, madly scribbling what would become, in print, the most clever, insightful and profound reflections on the place we call home. From her first days as a reporter to her days on the city council and beyond, Jean Godden and her ubiquitous notebook have been the essential guide to life in Seattle, the one constant in a city that is always about to change. Enjoy!

Leonard Garfield, Executive Director
Museum of History and Industry
August 2018

Preface

In the West people ask newcomers: "What do you do?" In the South, they ask, "Who are your people?" It's my job to answer both questions as well as a third: "Who am I?"

I was born Jean Hecht into a nomadic military family. My father Morey made maps and charts for the U.S. government. My mother Bunny used her English degree to teach Chicago telephone operators how to pronounce numbers ("ni-YUN") although she sometimes found work teaching William Shakespeare to back country teens who spoke almost pure Middle English.

Wherever my dad's assignments took him, we followed. I was born in Stamford, Connecticut, a town where we stayed all of three months. Most of our travels were in the southeast United States where dad and a large survey party completed preliminary maps for the Tennessee Valley Authority.

We lived in hotels, tourist homes, tents, and trailers. Sometimes we camped in city parks. I remember feeding the captive monkeys and alligators in small town zoos in West Virginia and Florida. My younger brother Harry arrived during those years, born in Hattiesburg, Mississippi. My mother cushioned a hotel dresser drawer with towels for his first cradle.

When I reached school age, our travels slowed down, a year here, a year there. But I still managed to attend 16 schools in a dozen states before I graduated from high school. During World War II, my father transferred temporarily from one military service, the U.S. Coast and Geodetic Survey, to another, the U.S. Army. He trained field artillery observation battalions at army bases in Mississippi, Missouri, Kentucky, and North Carolina. One battalion he trained was captured— an entire battery assassinated—during the Battle of the Bulge. As the war wound down, dad was assigned to Fort Sill, Oklahoma, to teach meteorology and technology, helping perfect the advances of radar.

After the war, dad returned to the Coast Survey and was ordered to Norfolk, Virginia, then to Seattle, Washington, a city that we had heard about from other service families, but had never seen. Dad would be based in Seattle, serving aboard survey vessels and charting waters in the Aleutian Islands. He later commanded a land-based survey party that charted waters on the North Coast of Alaska.

Dad had already reached Seattle in June 1950, when I graduated, age 17, from high school in Norfolk, and when my mother taught her last math class (a neat trick for a woman who could write a sonnet but could never balance a checkbook). My brother, mother, and I packed our bags once again and drove across the country to Seattle. On a glorious August morning, we crossed the Floating Bridge, referred to by some locals as the "eighth wonder of the world," and drove through the Mount Baker tunnel marked "Portal to the North Pacific." It seemed a wonderful, star-crossed omen.

By the time we reached Seattle, mother's list—the one she had kept throughout her married years—reached 116. That's the number of different cities and towns where we had lived.

We first stayed in the Ravenna neighborhood with the Johnsons, another Coast Survey family. For me, that visit would last only a couple of weeks, since I had enrolled in Northwestern University, my parent's alma mater. The campus in Evanston, Illinois, was close enough to grandparents with whom I could spend holidays, better than spending scarce tuition dollars to travel two days each way on a train ride to Seattle.

In my introductory weeks in Seattle, I formed early impressions. The city was smashingly beautiful: Lake Washington, the Sound, the hills, the tall trees, and the framework of mountains. It was simply the most spectacular place I had ever seen. The city was remarkably clean and welcoming after the crowded East Coast. The Seattle cityscape, although confusing, had much to offer even a short-time visitor.

I learned to know Ravenna Park and travel along its trails with Thora Johnson, daughter of our temporary hosts. I quickly learned that fashions current in Virginia had yet to reach Seattle, a city that had a non-style of its own. I gaped at young women who wore bobby socks and sandals, who wore their skirts wide and short, who mixed plaid with stripes and looked like fugitives from a second-hand sale. But I was mightily impressed with their immediate acceptance of a stranger, even one with a slight southern accent and outlandish (to them) clothing. The hell of moving around the country is that you are never dressed right.

I would spend two years studying at Northwestern's Medill School of Journalism and working on the *Daily Northwestern* before returning home to Seattle. I lucked into a summer job as news editor for the *University District Herald*, a free community weekly. By then, my mother had bought the family's first house in the Bryant neighborhood and I took the bus each weekday morning to my newspaper job. Instead of returning to school at Northwestern, I stayed on at the *Herald* thinking I could complete my journalism degree less expensively at the University of Washington.

Be careful making plans; they sometimes go awry. I fell in love with and married Robert (Bob) Godden, a commercial artist who sometimes worked at the *Herald*'s printing plant. We soon bid good-bye to my parents who were off on their next assignment in Washington, DC, and to my brother, off to enroll in the University of Arizona.

My newspaper career was put on hold after the arrival of my first son and then another. It wasn't until our children reached school that I was able to return to complete my college degree: Not in journalism, because by then the school had become the Department of Communication.

In the interim, I had worked part-time as my husband's book-keeper, took freelance jobs, and worked on community projects. I was propelled into activism following a disastrous double school levy failure in Seattle. When my elder son's kindergarten class was cancelled, I helped organize a cooperative kindergarten. That led to my election as PTA president. I became an active member of the League of Women Voters, Citizens Against Freeways, and the Seattle Municipal League.

After finally getting that elusive communications degree in 1974, I found a job at the *Seattle Post-Intelligencer* where I worked as an urban affairs reporter, editorialist, editorial page editor, business editor, restaurant critic, and then as a city columnist. In the 1990s, the *Seattle Times* made an offer I couldn't refuse and I took my column to the region's largest daily paper.

On July 31, 2003, after 20 years as a city columnist, I abruptly quit my job to run for Seattle City Council. To my astonishment (and the surprise of others) I was elected, defeating five male challengers and an incumbent. Over time I chaired the Energy and Environment, Finance and Budget, Parks and Recreation and Waterfront committees as well as committees overseeing public utilities, libraries, and gender equity.

Today—some would say it's about time—I am semi-retired. I still get to write for *Westside Seattle*, a combination of four community weeklies. I seem to have come full circle. I started my career at a community newspaper and now I enjoy writing opinion pieces for a respected weekly.

What could be better than having two careers, one as a witness recording city history being made and a second one participating in making that history? Seattle is my adopted city, the only one where I have roots. It is a city that has gone from a remote waystation, little known on the world stage, to a leader in civic and national affairs. No longer do people ask if Seattle is near Nome or if you can see Anchorage from here. What is happening in Seattle today shapes the world tomorrow.

Introduction:
My Assignment

It's December 21, 2015, three days after I closed the door of my City Hall office for the last time. I wake before dawn, shower, start to dress for shopping—the Christmas holiday is only four days away—and I collapse. I am out stone cold, crumpled onto the floor of my upstairs bathroom.

The crash of my body striking the floor alerts my son Jeff, who is downstairs in the kitchen brewing coffee. He rushes upstairs. Discovering that I have passed out, he picks up his cell phone and calls 9-1-1. His call sounds to me like a far distant echo.

I pry open my eyes, unbelieving, as I watched six Seattle firefighters crowd into my narrow bathroom—five men and a woman. They help me into a semi-upright position and, thankfully, into my bathrobe.

"Does it hurt?" they ask.

"Hurts to breathe."

"How badly on a scale of one to ten?"

"At least a seven." It hurts even to talk.

"We're taking you to emergency," says one firefighter. "Where do you want to go?"

"Northwest Hospital." I seem to remember that's where my doctor goes.

The firefighters wrap me in a rubberized sheet, lift and carry me one step at a time down the steep stairs to the front door, out into the cold and the still blue-black December morning. They hoist me onto a gurney and into the Medic One van. I marvel at how effortlessly they transport me. But I still struggle with the pain of breathing. It's like a clamp tightening across my chest just below the elastic of my brassiere.

Although only half aware, I can tell we're headed, sirens wailing, not to Northwest Hospital, but toward the University of Washington emergency room. It's not where I expect to go. But it's closer to home and easier to navigate at 7:00 a.m. on a weekday.

I am now in Emergency, under bright, searing lights. I realize I am being rolled onto an examining table, tended by a well-trained army checking vital signs and asking more questions. Had I hit my head? Traveled recently? Taken a fall?

No to all of the above. But it still hurts to breathe. And I am beginning to worry that Christmas is that much closer. Although I am not wearing a watch and have no idea how long I've been here, I realize that I am not getting my shopping finished. Could I please be examined and leave?

I am ignored; it doesn't work that way. I drift off and gain consciousness in a draped room, seated beside a nurse, a crisp professional, who asks more questions. Then, finally, I am surrounded with people in hospital scrubs who want me to sign a permission slip for an angioplasty, a procedure that will involve an incision in my groin and the threading of instruments to examine my heart and arteries.

I sign awkwardly and am given something by mouth that makes me light-headed and woozy. I am aware of bright, glaring lights and masked figures bending over me. There is music playing somewhere, not my style, but pleasant enough. Although I have trouble focusing, I glimpse a screen to my left with what looks like a branching tree. The branches wobble and wiggle.

"There it is," says one of the masked crew. "Let's take care of it."

"Got it," says another. Through the fog, I wonder what they've got.

Later I am back in the curtained room. A woman arrives with a machine. She sits close beside me and asks me to breathe in, breathe out. I am being checked for something and the task seems never ending. Whenever I take a deep breath, I still feel tightness.

Finally, a slim male doctor arrives, shakes my hand and tells me that they have inserted a "stent" into an almost blocked artery. This was my problem and I may soon be good to go. Except that, wait a minute, there may be something else, something spotted by the woman and her machine. They tell me that they are finding a hospital bed for me, but first I must be inserted into a whale-shaped machine for an MRI scan.

For an hour my arms are locked over my head and I can breathe only through my mouth. Afterward, to my surprise, I am told the artery repair was only a partial fix. It appears I have blood clots in my left lung. These are potentially life-threatening, but I will be given medicine that will cause them to dissolve.

There is nothing like being rolled into a hospital bed and told that you have been rescued, teetering at the brink. And you now must be grateful for medicine that will have (and does have) all sorts of uncomfortable side effects. But rejoice. You have been shot at and missed, at least for a time.

Tucked into a hospital room, plugged into monitors and IVs, lying awake to the clatter of hospital noises that long night, it strikes me that it is late, much later than I had thought. It's not just Christmas shopping that I have not completed. It is writing down the stories, the ones that I always meant to tell. I had planned to tell those stories but haven't gotten around to it.

I had never told the hidden story about Gov. Dixy Lee Ray and the Mount St. Helens eruption that killed 57 souls. Nor had I written about Mayor Charley Royer's initial response when the Greek freighter rammed the West Seattle Bridge. I also had missed telling the inside story of Mayor Norm Rice's heroic efforts to squelch a blatantly false rumor. If not for that rumor Rice might have been governor.

On a personal level, I had never fully confided why I decided to leave the best job in the world: writing a newspaper column. Why I had found myself, one of six challengers, running for office, a long shot against a popular incumbent city councilmember.

It is these stories that now—released from the aroma of hospital disinfectants and the tether of IV tubes—I am finally ready to tell.

The tales that follow are based on my own notes, ample files, recollections, and personal experiences. Quite simply, these are the stories that I failed to tell.

For example, I neglected writing about the staff "cool-down party" held the night that the *Seattle Post-Intelligencer* moved from Sixth and Wall Street to a building on the waterfront. The staff wanted to hold a big party in the newsroom, but *P-I* comptroller Bill Cobb thought there might be alcohol (there was) and refused to assume the liability.

We rented the nearby Catholic Seamen's Club where we celebrated by giving mock awards to our colleagues for their foibles—to columnist

Joel Connelly for his plague-infected desk and to over-eager reporter John Hessburg for his newsroom tantrums.

Signal event of the evening was when *P-I* publisher Virgil Fassio asked reporter Mary Lynn Lyke to dance. To everyone's surprise, Fassio, a chunky, one-time Penn football player, was an accomplished dancer. As he expertly tangoed across an uneven floor, he nimbly dipped his partner. Then he stumbled. He dropped Mary Lynn and landed squarely on top of her.

It was one of those bewildering moments when you don't know whether to laugh, spit, or stifle. I remember Fassio's fatalistic response. He said, "Whatever else anyone remembers about tonight, this will be the takeaway." He was right.

There have been other defining moments—both high and low—and here they are, forever in my memories.

1

It Was a Secret Plot, 1962

My editor once assigned me to interview Bud Clark, the colorful tavern owner who had been elected mayor of Portland, Oregon. As a *Seattle Post-Intelligencer* columnist, I was just doing my job that day in 1987. I had been assigned a Sunday newspaper article on distinctions between Portland and Seattle, two rivals often called "sister cities."

When I asked Clark about differences, the gregarious mayor—known for posing as a flasher for an "Expose Yourself to Art" poster and for riding a bicycle to work while shouting "Whoop! Whoop!"—didn't hesitate.

"The World's Fair," he said. "Seattle had a fair in 1962 and we didn't. It made all the difference between Seattle and Portland."

Clark put his finger on the watershed moment that separated the two cities. That moment was 25 years earlier when Seattle opened the Seattle World's Fair, a twentieth-century exposition dubbed "Century 21." Putting on the fair was a gutsy move for Seattle. Even today, nearly 60 years later, it is hard to fathom how Seattle could manage a major world's fair. Even harder to imagine was the little-known city undertaking a fair devoted to the latest in space-age technology.

It started with a brainstorm from Seattle City Councilman Al Rochester. The councilman had fond memories of the 1909 Alaska-Yukon-Pacific (A-Y-P) Exposition held in his youth. That successful fair took place just 10 years after the "Ton of Gold" had arrived in Seattle from the Yukon. The successful A-Y-P Exposition celebrated Seattle as the gateway to Alaska and left behind a tangible legacy, the backbone for the University of Washington campus.

Councilman Rochester's bright idea was to hold another major fair 50 years after the A-Y-P. As it turns out, he missed the mark. The mid-century fair didn't quite come together by the 1959 anniversary date. But come together it did, postponed while Rochester lined up the necessary support. He got early backing from a core group of Seattle businessmen. Their efforts were bolstered by an enthused public, the state legislature, and a generous congressional grant.

Most remarkable was the unexpected but welcome official sanction by the Bureau of International Expositions (BIE) in Paris, France. The bureau likely had not even heard of Seattle, Washington. Meanwhile, New York City was also in the running for official world's fair sanction. Given the Big Apple's prominence, that city seemed assured of winning. Only one U.S. city could be officially designated.

Apparently the BIE members thought Seattle was a suburb of the other Washington, the United States capital. Gossipy stories held that the New Yorkers were arrogant and full of themselves while the Seattle petitioners were polite, humble, and appealing. For whatever reason, Seattle miraculously won out over New York City's competing bid. Seattle's science-themed fair would be the first exposition held on American soil in 22 years.

Once Seattle received official international sanction, the difficult work of obtaining money and land got underway. The World's Fair Commission, appointed in 1955 by Gov. Arthur Langlie, considered several sites including Sand Point (a Naval Air Station on Lake Washington), Fort Lawton (an Army base overlooking Puget Sound), Duwamish Head at the northern point of West Seattle, Lake Union, and First Hill. The commission finally decided on a centrally located, 74-acre chunk of land surrounding the city's Civic Auditorium and Ice Arena.

The site, selected and cleared by eminent domain, was a plot of land that early settlers had called "Potlatch Meadows." Settlers believed that it had once been the scene of Native American tribal festivals. The pioneer David Denny family, who farmed the land, merely knew it as "the prairie."

After site selection, money became the next critical issue. Seattle voters approved funding for Al Rochester's exposition, saying yes to a $7.5 million bond issue. But subsequent attempts to interest the state legislature came to naught.

Then, after the 1956 election of another Al—this time Gov. Al Rosellini—the state voted to match Seattle's funds. To sweeten the pot, Sen. Warren Magnuson managed to convince Congress to appropriate $12.5 million. Prominent businesses also lined up, supplying funds needed for maintenance and operation. Getting the money together, difficult as it was, turned out to be one of the easier tasks. Next came the hard work of lining up exhibits and entertainment.

Restrictive company policies prevented the Boeing Company, the region's largest employer, from making direct contributions to the effort. Nevertheless, plans were underway for Boeing to build a "Spacearium." The Boeing attraction would take fairgoers on a make-believe 60-quintillion-mile (think 18 zeroes) trip through the stars.

The Spacearium, one of the fair's biggest attractions, was no sure thing. At first, Boeing President William Allen, never an easy sell, had stubbornly resisted. He predicted the fair would turn into a financial disaster. It took fast talking from his friend William Street, Century 21 Exposition Inc. chairman, to change Allen's mind.

To clear the land for the fairgrounds, more than 200 homes and structures—13 square blocks—were condemned and demolished. From the very beginning, planners were clear about their intention that the fair's major structures would not be torn down afterwards. Those buildings would become a permanent civic asset.

In fact, planners secretly believed that they were actually building what some called "a Civic Center disguised as a World's Fair."

It is no wonder that Century 21 planners had that long-range vision. While fair preparations were underway, then Seattle Mayor Allan Pomeroy simultaneously appointed a Civic Center Committee. He laid out the task. As quoted in a *Seattle Times* story, Pomeroy stated, "Seattle's community facilities for sports, cultural activities, convention and public administration are most inadequate. Founders and early settlers moved entire hills to make a city. Certainly we can solve the problems a civic center would entail."

The underlying goal—to have the fair's assets double as an enduring civic asset—undoubtedly helped fuel enthusiasm. It also led to the addition of the Space Needle. Eddie Carlson, president of the World's Fair Commission, hatched that idea when he and his wife, Nell Carlson, were dining at a restaurant atop a TV tower in Stuttgart, Germany.

Well known in Seattle is the story of how Carlson picked up a cocktail napkin and sketched his notion for a World's Fair structure, a saucer-like shape attached to a stick-like tower. Back home, he told others he couldn't stop thinking that Century 21 ought to have "a restaurant in the sky."

Carlson's idea, however, was not instantly popular. First he tried to interest architects, some of whom scoffed at the proposal, likening the design to a phone pole wearing a sombrero or a pylon in a top hat. Before Carlson's dream could take shape, he had to enlist visionaries like University of Washington architecture professor Victor Steinbrueck and architect John Ridley. The pair worked to develop the graceful sheaf-like structure. Backup came from architect John Graham, a man with the right resume. He had already designed a revolving restaurant in Hawaii.

In retrospect, Carlson's Space Needle seems a perfect metaphor for the times. At 605 feet, it would then be the tallest structure on the West Coast. Pointed skyward into the clouds, the Needle was a symbol of Seattle's unstoppable spirit.

But before Carlson's vision could get underway, there first came a flat-out rejection by the three King County Commissioners. (This was several years before King County would elect councilmembers by district.) The thrift-conscious triumvirate turned thumbs down.

There were other obstacles. One citizen, Fred McCoy, wrote the city's Board of Public Works asking what would happen if the city was obliged to take over the building because of failure on the part of the lessee to make the project pay. We would then be stuck, in McCoy's words, "with a 550 [sic] foot high white elephant."

Joseph Gandy, president of Century 21 Exposition, wrote to Seattle Mayor Gordon Clinton and City Council President David Levine pressing them to disregard any such concerns. Gandy urged the city to approve the construction. Time was precious if the Space Needle were to be up and running in time for the fair.

Meanwhile Carlson refused to give up. He turned to five private investors, among them Howard Wright, who would sign on as the needle's contractor. The investors set up a private corporation and bought a small piece of land, once the site of a city fire station. They broke ground on April 17, 1961, just 52 weeks before the fair's opening. It would be a race against time and a real gamble, since there were still naysayers who thought the hastily constructed 605-foot Space Needle might end up leaning like the Tower of Pisa.

It was no accident that the 1962 exposition had adopted a strong science theme. On October 4, 1957, the Soviet Union launched Sputnik, beating the United States into space. The Soviet space shot fueled the space race, which provided a timely boost for the fair's science and future-based theme, "Man into Space." The fair's logo was an oval with an arrow pointed upwards into the heavens—the male Mars symbol.

Given the gender inequity of the 1950s and '60s and the fair's manly theme, it was no surprise that women were relegated to lesser roles. Planners were overwhelmingly men; cheerleaders were mainly women.

There was only one high-profile female role. That role involved showmanship. World's Fair planners were told that the fair, to be a success, must provide entertainment, especially at night. The fair planners announced the fair would have a Show Street, with entertainment that was "naughty but nice." There would be song and dance reviews, girlie shows, and nudity (gasp!) would be allowed.

Nudity in Seattle? What a surprising concept. At the time, the city still had a Board of Theater Supervisors, responsible for reviewing movies and making sure that films were family appropriate before they could be shown within city limits. In the approved movies, there were no double beds, not even for married couples.

On a day when the fair's campus was in various stages of construction and the iconic Space Needle had almost topped out, fair officials awarded Show Street's major nightclub contract to a complete unknown. Who had ever heard of Gracie Hansen, a brash fireplug of a woman from Morton, Washington? In her small hometown, she was known for putting on lively musical reviews for the parent-teacher association. By any estimate, it was a thin credential for an international exposition.

Most officials who met with Hansen during ramp-up to the fair were dubious if not disapproving. A heavy-set woman, Hansen was loud in speech and in dress. She knew how to attract the eye with her flamboyant outfits, some dripping with feathers and rhinestones.

Model Donna Rydberg, adult-entertainment impresario
Gracie Hansen, and milliner John Eaton (who created
Rydberg's headpiece), onstage at the Century 21 ground-
breaking event, 1961. *MOHAI, Donna Rydberg Fashion
Modeling Album, 2012.38.34*

My late husband Bob Godden was one of the ad men charged with
promoting Hansen's enterprises at the fair. He came home, describing
his first meeting with Hansen. He said, "I picked the quietest, darkest
corner of the restaurant [Clark's Red Carpet] hoping no one would
spot us or overhear us."

Bob's partner, Ross Swift, was no prude. But even he complained,
"It couldn't have been more embarrassing if I'd been having lunch with
a madam from a cheap bordello." Godden and Swift had earlier been
picked to design and produce an official World's Fair coloring book, one
of the many souvenirs that would help promote and finance the fair.

But if Swift and Godden were put off by Hansen's appearance, they couldn't help being beguiled by Hansen's enthusiasm. She grew almost magically from her small-town background into her impresario role. She soon announced that Barry Ashton, one of the nation's top showmen, would be producing shows at her nightclub, dubbed "Paradise International." Her "Nights in Paradise" review, featuring bare-breasted showgirls, topless but stationary (that was the city's compromise rule), attracted sold-out crowds.

Key to the success at Paradise International was scheduling quality vaudeville acts. In fact, one critic, when asked for his reaction, never mentioned the risqué display of so many braless bosoms. In press accounts, he concluded, "Well, there was this good dog act."

Hansen's Paradise International wasn't the sole adults-only entertainment on Show Street. "Girls of the Galaxy," a show that encouraged patrons to take photos of unclad young women, quickly ran afoul of the legendary Board of Theater Supervisors. Visible behind transparent panels on Show Street, the barely-clad Galaxy performers could be seen beckoning patrons to come inside. Rowdier passersby responded with loud shouts and unprintable remarks. When he learned of excessive shimmying and shaking by the show girls, Ewen Dingwall, the fair's general manager, immediately shut Galaxy down.

The shocked Dingwall decreed there would be "no lewd, immoral or obscene behavior, no bumps and grinds." The Galaxy producer promised to revise the show and reopen it. But before revision and official approval, a handful of performers decided to throw caution aside and reopen anyway. Fair officials fought back. They countered with an electrical shutdown, leaving the rogue show's staff to rely on makeshift lighting. The show went on with flashlights and lanterns.

The Galaxy battle provided gossipy grist for the Seattle newspapers that were carrying detailed daily reports on events at the fairgrounds. Eventually, compromises were made: The Galaxy showgirls agreed to don filmy brassieres, and a fire-eating act was added to the lineup. The show went on but closed weeks early due to financial losses.

Among other Show Street attractions was "Peeps," a mostly static show that featured models in various stages of undress engaged in mundane activities such as grooming, dressing, reading and knitting. Patrons declared that the show was scarcely worth the price, "boring" in fact.

More successful on Show Street was an uncensored puppet show, Les Poupees de Paris. The wooden puppets had more latitude to stray from the city's decency standards than flesh and blood performers. Apparently nothing said Century 21 like nude marionettes that could intermingle, assuming postures not permitted to live performers.

Century 21's scrappy, starry-eyed founders believed the Seattle World's Fair would put the little-known western city on the map. They were right. There's no question they had a success on their hands. Limited by the international bureau to a mere six-month run, the fair drew 10 million visitors and earned an unexpected profit. It was a watershed moment for the city.

The fair was a personal success for my own family as well. My ad-man husband Bob and his partner Ross Swift participated in the fair's marketing and public relations. Besides the official coloring books (the women are drawn wearing my duck's-ass hairdo), they also produced ads, flyers, and even punch-out hats and masks for attractions like the Alaska exhibit and the oversized Paul Bunyan Cake display.

My young sons and I made a dozen trips to the fair, partly for our own pleasure and partly guiding family visitors. We squeezed into the Bubbleator, the giant plexiglass elevator that took us to the "World of Tomorrow." A silver-suited Bubbleator operator managed overflow crowds of 100 people at a time, advising us to "step to the rear of the sphere." We viewed an imagined "city of the future" with jetports, gyrocopters, electric autos, farmlands covered with climate-controlled plastic domes, and the marvels of communication that "even a child can operate."

Across the fair's campus, we rode the high-speed Monorail and traveled to the Space Needle's observation deck. We ate in the revolving restaurant where we could view the constantly changing scenery. And no trip with children along could avoid the Gay Way rides, including the Wild Mouse, the fair's signature roller coaster.

We relished the United States Science Exhibit with its soaring arches and the special section for young people called "Doing Science" where the boys tried their hand at simple experiments. There were pavilions from around the world: Great Britain with a wall showing the progress of man "conquering" his environment, exhibits

Next morning bright and early they see the high speed monorail which will take them from downtown
Seattle to the fair grounds in just **90 seconds!**

Visiting family gazes in awe at the Monorail (note that Mom's hairstyle is modeled on my own 1962 coif). From *Official Century 21 Coloring Book: All About the Seattle World's Fair* (50th Anniversary Edition, 2012), story and pictures by Ross Swift and Bob Godden. *Author's collection*

from the European Communities, ceramic displays from the Republic of China, and exotic exhibits from Peru, the United Arab Republic, Japan, and Canada. The world had come to us in Seattle.

Pulling off a financially successful fair was a landmark in Seattle's relatively short history.

The repurposed grounds of the World's Fair did indeed become the civic center that city leaders had longed to create. Through succeeding years it has continued as a real magnet for arts and cultural activities. It has provided entertainment ranging from rock bands to the Seattle Opera, from the Beatles and Pearl Jam to Wagner's Ring Cycle and the Pacific Northwest Ballet's *Nutcracker*. Every year, tens of thousands gather on the grounds for an all-out arts party, an end-of-summer event called Bumbershoot.

Two icons, the privately owned and managed Space Needle (now the city's most recognized symbol) and the dated but still popular Monorail are the fair's most obvious legacies. The refurbished International Fountain remains a powerful anchor along with the two theaters, the Playhouse, and the later-added Bagley Wright Theatre.

Mainstays include the fair's repurposed Coliseum, long dubbed the KeyArena. The Coliseum once housed the Seattle Sonics basketball team that, although now departed, helped draw Seattle fully into major league sports. Today the Coliseum's days as a sports mecca seem far from over. The city has approved plans submitted by the Oak View Group—a group of sports investors—to redevelop and expand the Coliseum, preserving its signature roof line. Oak View is pursuing a National Hockey League expansion team and, with luck, another professional basketball team.

The Science Center with its signature arches draws world-class exhibits like King Tut and the ancient Chinese warriors. Meanwhile, the repurposed Armory Building sates appetites with food from more than a dozen outlets.

The nonprofit Museum of Pop Culture (MoPOP), initially established by Microsoft co-founder Paul Allen as the Experience Music Project (EMP), occupies a futuristic Frank Gehry-designed building. The architecture and coloring of the building has prompted some to say that "it looks as if the Space Needle doffed her clothes and forgot to pick up them up."

It's no wonder that when residents measure city events, they often use the Century 21 exposition as their yardstick, saying, "It happened before the fair" or "right after the fair." Century 21 served as a maturing moment for a city outgrowing its small town ways.

2

Ramps to Nowhere, 1956–1972

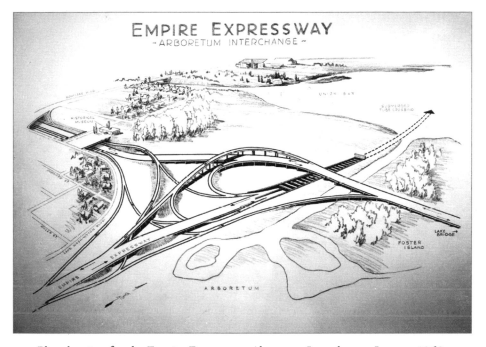

Plan drawing for the Empire Expressway Aboretum Interchange, January 1960. *Seattle Municipal Archives, Item 63490*

It all started in 1956 when Seattle voters approved the "Empire Expressway." The name came from its route along Empire Way, a Seattle arterial named for railroad magnate James J. Hill, the man they called "the Empire Builder." Later Empire Way would be renamed to honor Dr. Martin Luther King Jr.

There was little opposition to the Empire Expressway at first. After all, it was the freeway-loving 1950s. Think Los Angeles and its elevated roadways soaring in all directions. If L.A. had high-flying freeways, so must Seattle.

The Washington State Highways Department sold the Empire Expressway as part of an ambitious plan designed to move transportation through the Seattle area. At that time, the department was busy completing Interstate-5, a freeway that sliced Seattle into fragmented halves. Like State Route 99 before it, I-5 would serve as the main route linking Mexico to Canada.

But if two north-south freeways knifing through the city's heart were such a good idea, some thought: Why not three? And so, along with a planned second Lake Washington Bridge (SR-520) at Montlake, the department barreled ahead with plans to connect the Empire Expressway to the 520 Bridge. The expressway would also connect to an expanded I-90, and likely to two more Lake Washington bridges (one parallel to state route 520 and one stretching from Matthews Beach to Kirkland). By then, there would be "need" for more east-west connections, an elevated Bay Freeway at South Lake Union, and another at Connecticut Street.

Talk about freeway madness. The highway builders had sectioned the city into rectangular grids. There seemed no way to stop the frenzy to pave over a large percentage of the long narrow city and its fragile terrain.

Enter a counterforce: Margaret Cary Tunks, a new Seattle resident who had arrived in 1963, fresh from Essex County, New Jersey. Margaret was the wife of Lehan Tunks, the University of Washington's new law school dean. Margaret herself had studied law although she never had gotten around to passing the bar. Instead she had been busy raising a family while watching Newark, New Jersey, sink into decay. Upper and middle-class families deserted Newark for the suburbs. She feared Seattle could be another Newark, on the brink of urban deterioration.

She wrote about her realization saying: "In 1968, we had just moved into a new neighborhood in Northeast Seattle when a neighbor asked us to go with him to a meeting at our school (Cedar Park in Lake City). A State Highway Department engineer would talk about a new freeway to be built through our area."

During the September 1968 meeting, Wallace Foster, the highway department speaker, showed maps of possible corridors for the new freeway. There were eight possible routes, labeled from "A" through "H." The highway he discussed that night was to become State Route

522, a new road from State Route 405 east of Bothell, around the end of Lake Washington and through the Lake City area of Seattle, past the Ravenna, Montlake, and Leschi neighborhoods, connecting with I-90 at Mount Baker.

"Who will use this new highway?" Tunks asked. Foster said 90 percent of the drivers would be people soon to be living in North Bothell and Woodinville. Asked how long this six- to eight-lane freeway would serve the area, Foster said that he expected the roads and bridges to reach full capacity "as soon as they were finished." He said a corridor hearing to determine the route would likely be held in December 1968 or January 1969.

Tunks and her neighbor looked at plan H and found that it went within two blocks of their homes. She was astonished. She couldn't believe that non-existent suburbanites were to be served by another enormous freeway. She resolved to find out more about the planned projects.

What she discovered was that the Empire Expressway had long been in the works. It was first proposed and funded by the 1956 city bond issue and then by a second bond issue in 1960. The city had already authorized acquisition of certain properties. Some of the affected homeowners were suing, hoping to push city planners to reroute the expressway through the University of Washington Arboretum. Meanwhile, arboretum supporters were also gearing up to defend the popular botanical park.

Tunks tried to understand how it all transpired. She later summed up the project in *Seattle Citizens Against Freeways*, a book she wrote and paid to publish in June 1999. She concluded, "The fault lay in the process by which transportation decisions were made. The city's planners were traffic engineers and the process was managing traffic, not transportation planning." As she pointed out, the traffic engineers merely measured present traffic and then predicted future needs by enlarging streets and building bigger ones with no regard for secondary effects.

These predictions and decisions made for the sake of transportation resulted in homes left vacant and deteriorating, and "for sale" signs blossoming along proposed routes in the Montlake and Ravenna neighborhoods.

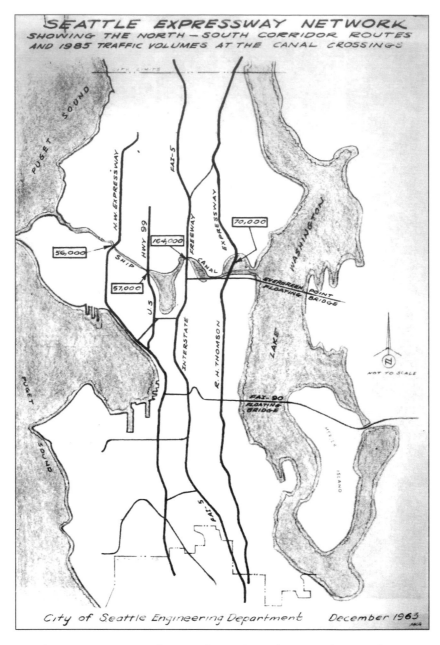

Seattle Expressway Network, December 1963, with proposed R. H. Thomson Expressway, between I-5 and Lake Washington. *Records of the Mayor, Box 40 Folder 12, Seattle Municipal Archives.*

The state, seemingly unstoppable, charged ahead with the Evergreen Point (SR 520) Bridge and built the soaring concrete pillars for the Arboretum Interchange—massive freeway ramps meant to connect with the Empire Expressway—at the north end of the Arboretum.

Hostility to the projects stirred in earnest in 1961 when the city began acquiring property in the expressway corridor. At that point, someone at the city had an idea designed to mitigate possible opposition: Why not make the Empire Expressway project more palatable by renaming it? Why not christen it the "R. H. Thomson Expressway" (or RHT) after Seattle's first city engineer? Thomson was a revered civil servant known for masterminding the city's water supply system, creating Seattle City Light, and taking down hills and filling mudflats. Thomson's massive regrades were among the largest land use projects in U.S. history.

Thus the highway's name was changed to honor a respected city figure. But there were no changes to soften the potentially devastating effects of the freeway juggernaut. It would likely rival the massive disruptions endured during the building of I-5.

Tunks continued her research on freeway plans, unearthing records from the past. She discovered a 1963 *Seattle Times* article that showed a map of a Seattle Central Business District (CBD) Plan. The headline read: "Freeway Pattern to Ease Traffic Problem for Suburban Residents." Development of the plan had been paid half by the city of Seattle and half by the Downtown Seattle Association, an organization of realtors, developers, and businesses.

A map accompanying the *Times* article showed a ring road around the city's business district. Even at that time, detractors had derided the plan, calling it "The Noose." Others sneered that what passed for transportation planning in the city consisted of "simply moving bottlenecks around."

The R. H. Thomson proposal, along with other grandiose transportation plans, had reached a critical point: The stage was now set for picking the corridor for these roads.

The Montlake community had been forewarned and was already strongly opposed to the expressway. Maynard Arsove, president of the

Montlake Community Club, had formed CARHT (Citizens Against R. H. Thomson) and was serving as its president. The Ravenna neighborhood, too, was alerted under its community club president Bill Frantilla. He joined forces with Arsove becoming CARHT vice president.

But the news of the highway's sweep was only just beginning to hit the Lake City area. Neighbors began to gather, seeking to understand what lay ahead and what, if anything, they could do about it. At the same time, the University of Washington Bureau of Community Development was helping Lake City residents visualize the future through an ad hoc citizen organization called LIFT (Lake City Improves for Tomorrow.)

Given that LIFT had more general community goals, Tunks and her new friends and allies (I had been recruited by then) thought that, rather than involving LIFT, it would be better to create a more narrowly focused anti-freeway organization. We swapped ideas about what to call it. Acronyms, some cute (like CURT for "Citizens Understand Rapid Transit") and some contrived (SCOOT for "Some Citizens Opt for Transit"), were rejected and we decided to call it what it was: Citizens Against Freeways or simply CAF.

CAF joined forces with CARHT to continue getting the word out. The result was a packed general meeting on December 11, 1968, with well-known speakers explaining transportation law, citizen rights, and critical environmental concerns. Tunks arranged for a special guest appearance by Sam Wood, editor of *Cry California*, a magazine dedicated to that state's preservation efforts. Wood would explain how San Francisco had successfully quashed the Embarcadero Freeway.

Prior to the evening meeting, Margaret Tunks and I settled into the plush lobby of the Olympic Hotel to greet Wood. Margaret was equipped with a homemade fruitcake (her friend Mrs. Dean Rusk's recipe) and a large serrated knife, virtually a machete. She intended to cut fruitcake slices for the reporters invited to a press conference at the hotel. With the oversized knife, we looked like a pair of hired assassins.

When he finally arrived, Wood had other ideas. He had packed a full bottle of Jack Daniel's whiskey in his luggage. He planned to offer it to the reporters and maybe take a sip himself. There was some con-cern—mostly Margaret's and mine—that Wood's talk at the meeting that night might be a casualty of too much Jack Daniel's.

The night of December 11 arrived. It was dark and stormy, but that didn't keep people away. They just kept coming until all the seats in Jane Addams auditorium were filled. It helped that just prior to the meeting, the *Seattle Times* had carried a scary story headed: "New Six-Lane Bothell Freeway Link." We also had a surprise windfall: a leaked copy of the highway department's Route 522 proposed route through Lake City. We were able to copy the pages and hand them out at the meeting.

Sam Wood's speech, unaffected by the press conference happy hour, was the high point of the evening. He concluded with a strong call to action: "What San Franciscans did opposing a destructive free-way, you can do also."

With thousands of citizens aroused and mobilized, Tunks started research into the Washington State Highway Department and its budget. The department had evolved almost as an independent arm of government, answering solely to the state legislature, rather than to the governor.

What Tunks discovered in Olympia was a nest of legislators oper-ating a powerful highway lobby that had wrested control of the state's highway budget. Their goal was either to enrich themselves through construction contracts or to curry approval for projects that bene-fited their individual legislative districts. Small wonder that one of them, a Redmond legislator and Eastside realtor, came to be known as "Asphalt Al" Leland.

The tug-of-war over the destructive R. H. Thomson Expressway would be waged unresolved for a dozen years. The battle outlasted four Seattle mayors and a couple of dozen city councilmembers, as well as three state governors. During that time, Tunks gained admira-tion for three-term Gov. Dan Evans, but had only negative opinions of his successor, Gov. Dixy Lee Ray.

In her book, Tunks writes, "Dan Evans was governor for three terms—12 years—and for all those years, one of his primary objec-tives was to establish a state department of transportation (DOT).

Transportation, like all other government departments, would then have a secretary chosen and appointed by the governor. For 12 long years, the highway lobby kept this legislation hostage, often pitting transportation reform against must-pass school funding bills."

When Ray took over as governor in 1977, Tunks scrambled to meet with Lou Guzzo, the ex-newsman who was serving as the governor's aide. She asked Guzzo for an appointment with the governor. This would not be their first meeting. During Tunks' undergraduate years at Mills College in Oakland, California, Dixy Lee Ray had been working there as a lab assistant in embryology. Asked what Ray was like back then, Tunks said, "I only remember that she handed out the dead cats."

Although Tunks arranged to meet with the governor, the appointment was abruptly cancelled. Despite her efforts, Tunks never did get an audience with Governor Ray. Tunks dismissed Ray as a "vituperative spokesperson for the highway lobby, swallowing their orders without attention to the facts."

Combative feelings were mutual. Governor Ray later went on record charging that Margaret Tunks had "singlehandedly delayed the construction of I-90 by 20 years." The charge was patently false since Tunks had only arrived in 1963, but the vitriol was not surprising. The pugnacious governor never needed an excuse for rancor. This, after all, was the woman who often took angry swipes at Warren Magnuson, the state's admired senior senator.

Tunks continued to focus her efforts on Olympia, setting up a desk outside the lawmakers' offices. She kept current files in a cardboard box atop the desk. (She would accumulate more than 100 such boxes during her anti-freeway advocacy.) Her expertise on federal and state highway legislation grew so vast that legislators often consulted her on fine points of federal and state transportation law, even when they were voting in opposition to her goals.

To disarm hostile legislators, Tunks resorted to wit and humor. For instance, when she rose to speak, she could always count on Rep. Red Beck, a powerful member of the highway lobby, to rise and leave. She wrote, "Next time I was called on, I rushed to the podium quickly and said, 'I am waiting for Representative Beck to leave before I speak.'" After that, Beck didn't bother to exit.

Tunks sometimes sought my help writing press releases. What I excelled at was translating Margaret-speak—lengthy legalistic phrases—into understandable lay language. She also made good use of cartoons drawn by commercial artist Dave Lefebvre, one of our Lake City allies.

Dave Lefebvre cartoon from Margaret Tunks' 1999 book *Seattle Citizens Against Freeways. Author's collection*

Believing that Dave's cartoons explained disastrous situations better than she could, she had the drawings distributed to legislators and reporters through the legislative mail room. Lefebvre depicted the folly of massive road building with drawings of asphalt belching machinery. Or he might show a family seated at a restaurant with the dad saying to the waiter: "We'll have one more round of highways and give the bill to my young son, here."

Tunks herself worked to enlist allies wherever she could. She fed stories to the press and was described by male reporters such as the *Seattle Post-Intelligencer*'s Shelby Scates as "a Lake City housewife and member of the League of Women Voters." But she actually was not aligned with the league. Despite Margaret's pleas, the politically powerful organization had flatly declined to take an active role combating freeways.

I can vividly recall one occasion driving past the league's Seattle offices on 18th Avenue with Margaret as a passenger. Margaret, a mild-seeming woman in middle years who was seldom profane, must have startled passersby when she leaned out the car window to yell, "Fuck you, League of Women Voters!"

Back in Seattle neighborhoods, the forces of CARHT and CAF continued fighting fiercely to oppose the R. H. Thomson and another runaway freeway, the Bay Freeway. The latter was a six-lane elevated roadway designed to solve the "Mercer Mess," the traffic weave from SR-520 towards the Seattle Center and Elliott Bay.

By the late 1960s, the anti-freeway movement was gaining momentum, both through public hearings and active citizen pressure. Interim Mayor Floyd C. Miller, appointed when Mayor James D'Orma "Dorm" Braman left to work for the Nixon administration, responded to the growing force. He appointed a special task force in May 1969 to review transportation decisions.

Miller introduced the task force, saying, "We are resolved in our feeling that Seattle must plan its transportation system to improve our urban environment. We want a balanced system to improve, not ruin, our neighborhoods."

During an August 28, 1969, public hearing at City Hall, CAF and CARHT proponents united with allies from the Central District to oppose a proposed 14-lane surface cut through the Mount Baker neighborhood. The neighborhood-destroying ditch was designed as part of Interstate-90, an approach to the Mercer Island floating bridge.

Front rows in the Seattle City Council chambers were packed with construction workers in hard hats who were backing more asphalt and more roads. In the council's back rows, citizen activists were seated side by side with leaders of the Black Panthers. From the Panthers, they heard calls to burn the city down if such a devastating swath cut through their neighborhoods. The citizen activists joined the outcry when the Panthers yelled "Burn, baby, burn!" There was little doubt they meant it.

A few months later a closed-door meeting was set up between the State Highway Commission, the newly elected mayor of Seattle, Wes Uhlman, and the Seattle City Council, led by President Charles Carroll. The semi-secret meeting brought forth an ultimatum known as "The Zahn Offer" (named for Transportation Commission Chair George Zahn). Substance of the offer was that Seattle must agree to a memorandum of understanding, approving a third Lake Washington Bridge (I-90) and the Bay Freeway or lose all state road funds.

Less was said about continued work on the R. H. Thomson. And small wonder. By the end of the 1960s, citizen pressure on the mayor and council had grown strong enough to persuade the council to remove the R. H. Thomson from the city's comprehensive plan. On June 1, 1970, the council essentially killed the project, never mind that bonds approved in 1960 for the Empire Expressway still remained on the books.

While pulling the plug on the Thomson Expressway, the Seattle City Council stubbornly resisted further pressures. The councilmembers pushed ahead with the Bay Freeway, tentatively approving plans for an aerial six-lane freeway—a twin for the Alaskan Way Viaduct—capping Mercer Street. In so doing, the council rejected a smaller four-lane alternative and totally ignored calls to jettison the project altogether.

Opponents, including CARHT and CAF, filed suit to stop the Bay Freeway. They argued that the project varied too much from the design that voters had approved for bonding in 1960.

On November 13, 1971, King County Superior Court Judge Solie Ringold agreed with lawyers arguing the case for CARHT and CAF. In his oral decision, Judge Ringold enjoined the city from building the Bay Freeway. In a written decision, he advised the city to send the matter back to the voters.

The mayor and council took his advice and referred both the Bay and Thomson Freeways to the ballot. The complicated two-part referendum went to the voters on February 8, 1972. The electorate voted to terminate the R. H. Thomson and said "no" to the Bay Freeway. The vote to kill the Thomson was 71 percent, decisively ending that project. The Bay Freeway was more hotly argued, pro and con. But it, too, was defeated with 55 percent opposed. The anti-freeway movement clearly had established legitimacy.

The R. H. Thomson Expressway was dead. But, ironically, the brutal concrete off-ramps of the Arboretum Interchange, built to connect SR-520 to the now dead freeway, remained. Those "ramps to nowhere" would serve as grim reminders of highway hubris for years to come. Interestingly, they also served a couple of generations of University of Washington students and others who used them for sunbathing, diving, dancing, and rubbernecking.

In 2016, a handful of the surviving citizens who stopped the pave-everything movement along with their heirs organized a non-profit known ARCH (Activists Remembered Celebrated and Honored). They have been trying to rescue a piece of the ramps to nowhere. Their goal: a single arch, four columns with a cross section, to serve as a memorial to the time when Seattle's grassroots activists won a giant victory.

ARCH is right in wanting to memorialize one of the great moments of Seattle history. The victory over the R. H. Thomson confirmed that citizens can triumph against government, can win when putting neighborhoods ahead of freeways.

ARCH's mission to save the ramps as a memorial gained support from the Seattle City Council and also from the University of Washington's Arboretum and Botanical Garden Committee. Earlier there had been pushback from the state Transportation Department, concerned with environmental decisions handed down during planning for a new SR-520. But now there seems to be agreement on all side that, when the 520 lid is completed, there will be a memorial marking the valiant fight waged by citizens for a dozen years.

Today there remain pleasant Seattle neighborhoods, a magnificent botanical garden, and quiet streets that would have been destroyed by the freeway. An entire swath of the city was saved from becoming a suburban throughway and citizens were empowered to oppose run-away freeway projects.

In the aftermath of the R. H. Thomson's demise, Margaret Tunks continued to work harder than ever to constrain I-90's planned 14 lanes and to make that route available to mass transit. Here she and her allies were partly successful. The route that would have contained so many lanes was narrowed, the cut through Mount Baker lidded, and provision made for rapid transit across I-90.

In 1993, weary of her fight as a full-time activist and suffering from debilitating arthritis, Tunks, a recent widow, moved to Southern California to be close to one of her sons.

Along with her went those hundred boxes of files. She used them as background for her 1999 book, *Seattle Citizens Against Freeways: Fighting Fiercely and Winning Sometimes.* Her conclusion: "Seattle can be saved only if the elected officials and the citizens care enough to save themselves."

From Margaret Tunks and her allies, we learned how important it is to maintain a balance between mobility and community. We also saw that a determined citizenry can prevail.

Seattle Post-Intelligencer building, 1948, Webster & Stevens photograph.
MOHAI Photograph Collection, 1983.10.16879.2

3

Patty Hearst and
Richard Nixon, 1974

The inch-high headline stored on the printer's stone in the *Seattle Post-Intelligencer*'s back shop read: "PATTY HEARST RESCUED." The headline, like advance obituaries written about celebrities still alive and kicking, hadn't been inked. Not yet.

In fact, when I first walked into the *P-I* as a new hire on February 11, 1974, Patty, the teenage Hearst heiress, had just been kidnapped from her Berkeley apartment the previous week. Before the "Patty Hearst Rescued" headline would be of any use, the Hearsts (owners of the *P-I*) would expend millions trying to rescue her. Meanwhile, Patty passed a year with a radical group known as the Symbionese Liberation Army (SLA) and shouldered a gun during a bank robbery.

Thus began my 17 years at the *Post-Intelligencer*, Seattle's morning newspaper. It was an unusually eventful year, starting with the Hearst kidnapping. Six months later I would be standing in the *P-I*'s newsroom, side by side with reporters and editors, my colleagues, watching on television as the president of the United States, Richard Nixon, resigned his office and walked to a waiting helicopter.

I will never forget that first year, nor that first day. I entered the *P-I* building at Sixth and Wall Street, my chest tight, all butterflies and goosebumps. The building was an Art Deco structure, solid as a rock. It supported the world on its sturdy shoulders, a three-story steel globe with revolving neon letters ("It's in the P-I") topped by a bald eagle, wings upstretched.

I walked in and found myself rubbernecking around the *P-I* lobby with its checked black and white marble floor. I was awed. The two-story lobby was dominated by bold Depression-era paintings (men at work in the forest and seashore) by noted artist Eustace Ziegler. Emblazoned on one wall were the words of Thomas Jefferson: "If left to me to decide whether we should have a government without news-papers or newspapers without a government, I should not hesitate to prefer the latter."

The day before my arrival, I had received a phone call from a woman who identified herself as Marge Cocker, assistant magazine department editor. She knew that I had recently applied to work at the *P-I*, listing a new University of Washington communications degree and my three years as news editor of the *University District Herald*, a free community weekly. Cocker was looking for someone to fill a temporary job editing the newspaper's Friday entertainment section.

As instructed I took the elevator to the second floor and found my way to the building's northwest corner, home to the editorial offices. My first encounter was a portly, tweed-jacketed fellow, cigar clamped firmly in his teeth. He was madly pounding away on an upright Royal typewriter. "Jack Sullivan," he introduced himself, not bothering to remove the cigar.

When I said I was trying to find Marge Cocker, he pointed to a centrally enclosed office. There I found Marge, a well-rounded woman dressed as casually as if she'd just arrived from her kitchen. The only occupant, she was seated comfortably behind one of the office's two paper-heaped desks.

"It's a pretty shitty thing to do, asking you to take this temporary job between editors," she confided. "But I figured that, since you'd worked at a community paper, you'd know how to do layout. You'll be talking to Archie over there by the window."

I took that as a dismissal and found Archie seated just outside Marge's office. He was a tower of a man, sandwiched into a too-small desk. He looked like a parent visiting his kid's kindergarten room.

"Archie Satterfield," he said, introducing himself. "I've been edit-ing 206—you know, the Friday entertainment section." He had a soft voice for a giant, a warm drawl—Midwest I thought—like an edu-cated ranch hand. He explained that I would be taking over as interim 206 editor for a few weeks while he, Archie, moved on to edit the Sunday book section.

Archie continued: "Bill Arnold—he's one of our newer employ-ees—is dying to move over to 206 and do the movie reviews. But he can't. Not yet. Not until they find someone to fill his job, editing letters and columns for the editorial page. He's stuck over there waiting for the editorial page editor to return from sick leave."

Archie offered me a long, detailed stream of advice. I learned that I was expected to ride herd on half a dozen critics and reporters who wrote for the Friday section. If their copy arrived late, I should reject it and fill news space with holdover or wire copy. I would edit, write headlines, and lay out the tabloid-sized pages, usually 24, and then supervise makeup in the composing room.

Archie added that, if a story didn't fit, I'd need to trim it, using one of my previously-honed skills: being able to read the metal type upside down and backwards. When approved, the type was fitted into metal matrixes, ready for stereotyping, the procedure used in the hot-metal technique of the times.

The technology mirrored what we used when I had edited the *University District Herald*, starting as a college dropout hired for the summer. Since then I had married, raised two sons and, once they were launched in school, I entered the University of Washington to earn a belated communications degree. By that time, my husband, a talented commercial artist, was suffering from a malady that we would later learn was multiple sclerosis. We knew that, if it were indeed MS, I might soon become the family's primary breadwinner.

That first week at the *P-I* gave me an opportunity to learn the lay of the land. The back shop and composing room where union printers made up the news pages was on the same floor, a block-long walk from the editorial offices. Stories were sent to the shop through ancient pneumatic tubes, cranky technology once used to move cash in large department stores.

Editors picked up proofs returned by tube or, if in a hurry, walked to the back shop. The editors used the proofs to measure stories and dummy them into page layouts.

The walk to the shop took you past the one-time women's section with its ever-changing name. No longer politically correct as a society or women's page, it was sometimes called "Features," sometimes "Lifestyle." One newsman, typically irreverent, noticed that the top women editors were middle aged. He wickedly suggested calling it "Change."

The executive editor's offices occupied the northeast corner of the building, positioned next to the "bullpen," a glassed-in meeting room where editors met daily to select news stories destined for the front page. The bullpen abutted the city desk with the managing editor and the city editor lodged a step up. They had a clear view of the newsroom reporters and of the horse-shoe-shaped copy desk with its central spot reserved for the copy chief, also known as "the dealer."

On most desks throughout the building, I could see ashtrays heaped with cigarette butts positioned next to thick coffee mugs. The mugs contained remains of the day's cheap Maxwell House brew, weak enough to see the cup's bottom in the morning, filled with semi-solid sludge by afternoon.

Doug Date, the head copy boy (later we'd call them "copy aides"), would brew an immense silver urn full each morning and collect, if he could, five dollars a head for the month. Worst deadbeats were newspaper stars like columnist Emmett Watson who never seemed to operate in a cash society.

More than once, you would see Watson put his hands into his pockets and come out empty. He'd tell Doug, "Fresh out. Catch me next payday."

The third floor housed the publisher's corner office, the advertising and circulation offices, as well as a large conference room used for editorial board meetings. There also was a cafeteria, presided over by Lois. She took orders while stirring the soup of the day, usually with a cigarette stuck in the corner of her mouth. Lois had help from a couple of colleagues, former employees of the Dog House, a nearby 24-hour, seven-day-a-week hangout, a favorite of barflies and visiting musicians.

"Who's the 'ham and over easy?'" shouted Ione, who waited tables wearing pink fuzzy slippers. "Easier on my dogs," she explained when asked. "Been abusing them for years."

The three floors of offices were positioned above the newspaper's high-speed rotary presses. The basement printing plant turned out the paper's seven morning editions, the bulldog (Saturday's early edition of the Sunday paper), and various supplements and special editions. The building was solidly built in anticipation of the vibrations and noise of the presses.

To those who worked there, there was no sweeter sound than the Niagara-Falls-like roar of the presses in action. It meant that once again, there was a miracle underway. Out of daily chaos, we had somehow produced a newspaper.

My first week on the job was both wonderful and terrifying. After learning my way to the restroom, I worked hard and yet I went home each day certain I had made enough errors to be fired the next morning. Hadn't used the pneumatic tubes correctly? Picked up the wrong proofs? Miscounted a headline?

And then there were the people.

Maggie Hawthorne, the paper's drama critic, arrived on a dead run. She looked as if she'd just gotten out of bed. She said, "I'm gathering details on the Ladies Musical Club story. I'll get it in tomorrow."

"Sorry," I said, remembering Archie's advice. "The deadline's today. I don't see how we can get something in after the pages are made up."

"We'll see about that," huffed Maggie and dashed off without another word. Was I even going to make it through the first week?

Our exchange must have been overheard by a roomful of reporters and editors in the northwest wing. I heard Jack Sullivan clear his throat. Meanwhile, Archie Satterfield was using a circular gauge to compute the depth of a picture and a pica rule to dummy in a blurb. I thought I might have caught a smirk on his face.

Frank Chesley, the all-powerful TV critic, offered a knowing smile. He had just arrived at his glass-enclosed office, the one he shared with Shelby Scates, the *P-I*'s veteran investigative reporter. Chesley had been helpful, showing me where office supplies were kept so that I now had my very own paste pot, ruler, and reporters' notebooks. He made a habit of using colorful profanity, almost to see if I'd blush. But I was hardly shaken. I had heard far worse when I worked as part-time bookkeeper at my husband's advertising agency.

Also in hearing range was Rick Cocker, Marge's son, employed as a copy aide while he worked his way through college. Rick's latest assignment was to wait in the hours-long gas station lines, refueling personal cars for the magazine editors. Gas shortages and the OPEC oil embargo had hit the Northwest hard. Drivers were forced to wait hours for a chance to refill their tanks.

Mike Conant, whose editorial page offices were across from the magazine operations, apparently had also been listening. Although busy with page proofs, he looked up and wagged a shaming finger. It didn't feel like a vote of confidence.

Despite a sinking feeling, I labored on, walking as if on eggs to the composing room. I did my best to make lighthearted comments to the printer working on the 206 magazine pages. Unbreakable union rules insisted that only printers were allowed to touch the metal type and over the years they had become better editors than those of us hired for the job.

"Cut the story there. You don't need that last graph," said Tommy Nelson, the printer assigned to 206 for the day. "It reads better without it." And he was right.

I felt better when I saw the pages take shape, thinking I might pull off the first week's work. That is unless Maggie Hawthorne, the unhappy drama critic, had reported me to some higher authority.

The next morning, despite a restless night, I showed up early hoping for the best. My first indication came when Marge Cocker beckoned me into her office.

After only a few days, I had discovered that Marge was that certain someone who, in most office cultures, made things happen. She had gone out of her way from the beginning to make me feel like one of the gang. It was like having a second mother, someone who insists on knowing "everything" about you and offers advice in your best interest.

"Heard you had a dust-up with Maggie," said Marge. "Wouldn't let it bother me. Everyone knows she plays fast and loose with deadlines. I think it ought to work in your favor, even if she does make a stink."

With scarcely a pause, Marge switched topics, saying, "By the way, did I understand that your husband's ailing and you're going to have to support the family? If that's the case, you'd better apply for Bill Arnold's job on the editorial page."

How did Marge know all this—had I told anyone? But it was just the right moment for me, a bit of sympathy and a timely suggestion. It was no wonder I'd heard people refer to Marge as "Mother Cocker." She took us under her wing, like it or not. And even the hard-bitten newsies appreciated her interest.

My first week's work was almost completed on Thursday morning; I had only to read and approve page proofs for Friday's 206, an easy enough task. After turning over the proofs to the back shop and buoyed by Marge's words, I strayed over near Archie's desk.

"Hope I'm not interrupting," I said. "But I thought you might know what I should do to get a shot at Bill Arnold's editorial page job."

"Just so you know," Archie said, "Ruth Howell, the editorial page editor, has been out for months. She's being treated for Hodgkin's disease. Mike Conant and Bill Arnold have been holding the editorial pages together. They work for Lou Guzzo, a former executive editor, who's nominally in charge. If I were you, I'd talk to Mike and ask for a crack at the job although ultimately it would be Ruth's decision."

I had heard of Mike who had sterling credentials working with Model Cities, a federal anti-poverty program, and then as the *P-I*'s city hall reporter. He seemed the very role model for the young, hard-bitten newsman whose byline had so often appeared over reports on city government.

It took most of my courage to stroll across the room to the editorial page offices, two glassed-in cubicles looking west across Fifth Avenue, and ask Mike if he had a moment. He said he'd have time to talk after he distributed the day's page proofs.

I had a nervous lunch in the cafeteria and then waited to see Mike. I told him I was temporarily editing the magazine section but was also very interested in Bill Arnold's job.

"What's your background?" he asked.

I told him about my years at the *University District Herald* and my new communications degree from the University of Washington. I said that I'd known Ruth Howell briefly while both of us were active in the League of Women Voters. Finally, I mentioned my work with Citizens Against Freeways, a group opposed to construction of the R. H. Thomson Expressway.

"That's not going to do you any favors with Ruth," Mike said darkly. "She's very big on better transportation. She lives on the Eastside and has lost friends in accidents on the Mercer Island floating bridge."

Mike explained that if hired I'd be responsible for editing letters to the editor, as well as laying out the op-ed page, writing headlines for syndicated columns, and editing volunteer op-eds. Did I think I was capable?

Mike finally said I should give the job a try. But he stressed that it would only be temporary, subject to Ruth's approval when she got back from sick leave.

Still it was something of a bright hope for me. I put in six weeks as temporary editor on the magazine before starting an editorial page try-out. Weeks after my start, Ruth Howell returned from her cancer treatment. She was looking exceptionally fit for a 54-year-old Hodgkin's survivor. She would come to work on a dead run, carrying a vintage Coach purse tucked under one arm like a football and itching to award kudos or brickbats depending on the look of the day's editorial page.

At first, she wasn't pleased with me, irritated at having a new staffer she hadn't selected. Eventually we became friends, close enough to write editorials together, Ruth at the typewriter and me suggesting phrases. We'd write all morning and then adjourn for lunch before checking proofs in the afternoon. Outdoing even the colorfully profane TV critic Frank Chesley, Ruth had a vocabulary calculated to make seafarers blush. She could use the "F" word in every part of speech, sometimes several times in a single sentence.

What a time to work on a daily paper. Crisis followed crisis. There were anti-Vietnam War marches; protests against the Shah of Iran; angry shouts and demonstrations on the sidewalk at Sixth and Wall; and a radical group known as the George Jackson Brigade detonating pipe bombs throughout the city.

On one of those violent days, a woman walked into the *Post-Intelligencer* lobby carrying a bottle of vodka and a gun. She managed to get off five shots before being subdued. One shot flew into the elevator just as the doors opened and the three occupants watched in open-mouthed horror. Luckily no one was hurt. Later reports identified the gun-woman's grievance: She had written a letter to the editor and it had not yet been published. As I was now editing the *P-I* letters to the editor, she might have been gunning for me.

The newspaper was fielding at least one bomb threat a week. No doubt some were genuine threats, but at least a few were phoned in by bored staffers. They relished waiting for the all clear at the Grove, a bar and restaurant across Wall Street.

"More letters!" shouted Jack Doughty, the irascible editor who would, on occasion, burst into the editorial page offices. He demanded shorter letters and more of them. Doughty was notorious for his harsh, unforgiving judgments of those who worked for him. Like the lieutenant he'd been in Korea and in the early days of the Vietnam War, he communicated with terse typewritten memos.

One memo to a reporter: "Bruce. I have now had a chance to view your 'new' hair style. And I fail to see any change has taken place. I suggest you ponder this whole situation seriously and consider what your future is going to be on this newspaper. J.D."

The year 1974 will be forever remembered as the year of Watergate. In March, seven senior White House aides, including John Ehrlichman and Bob Haldeman, along with Attorney General John Mitchell, were indicted for their roles in the Watergate break-in. By then, I was deep into the new editorial page job, trying to keep up with fast-breaking events.

I would no sooner send a syndicated column to the shop—perhaps authored by Jack Anderson, Tom Wicker, Mary McGrory, or Patrick Buchanan—than new developments would render the opinion obsolete. Under union rules, I couldn't touch the metal type, so it became my role to direct the printers to dump freshly-set but quickly outdated columns into the "hell box" where the type was remelted into new ingots.

In July the Supreme Court handed down a stunning ruling: President Nixon couldn't withhold tapes recorded in the Oval Office and must surrender them to the special prosecutor.

Shortly after that bombshell, there showed up on the stone in the back shop, right next to the premature "PATTY HEARST RESCUED" headline, an anonymous two-column editorial headlined: "Nixon Must Resign." That was a pretty gutsy statement, especially for a Hearst newspaper.

While the Hearst Company did oversee national political policies, it allowed latitude to local dailies as long as the New York office received fair warning. The unsigned editorial, clear and well written, was sitting there, ready to run. At first, I thought the mysterious editorial might have been written by my boss Ruth Howell since it echoed her convictions. But later it became apparent that it was the work of Bill Sieverling, one of the newsroom's most thoughtful city editors, a newsman with a passion for politics and civic activism.

The strong and lucid statement was destined never to run. Once again fast breaking events passed it by, as they had so many columns written about Nixon and Watergate. Why didn't the gutsy must-resign editorial appear? We may never know. The *P-I*'s managing editor, Jack Doughty, who had won a bitter power struggle replacing former editor Lou Guzzo, may have vetoed it. Or Bill Sieverling himself may have had second thoughts.

Instead, on August 8, 1974, staffers flooded into the newsroom to face the TV monitors. As we watched, Richard Nixon announced that he would resign the following day, August 9, with Gerald Ford, his recently appointed (post-Spiro Agnew) vice president, taking office. Soon afterward, Ford pardoned Nixon, giving rise to an unusual political era when the safest credentials for office were a lack of experience. Watergate would impact national elections, and Jimmy Carter, little-known outside Georgia, would soon be elected president. The desire for new faces also impacted political races in Seattle and Washington State.

The Nixon-must-resign editorial ended up in the hell box, along with so many opinions before it. Not so the Patty Hearst story. The "Patty Rescued" headline would remain in the composing room, gathering dust month after month until Hearst finally was found. She was taken into custody on September 18, 1975, in San Francisco, following an all-out FBI effort that involved a massive shootout, fatal fire, and a nationwide hunt. The granddaughter of newspaper magnate William Randolph Hearst was charged with bank robbery and other crimes. Her trial proved as sensational as the rest of her saga. Despite claims of brainwashing, the jury found her guilty. She was sentenced to seven years in prison, but was pardoned after two years by then president Jimmy Carter. Patty Hearst later married and had a family, vanishing into quiet East Coast society where she exhibits pedigreed dogs and no doubt receives profits from the Hearsts' media empire.

By the time the Patty Hearst headline ran, I had worked almost two years on the *Seattle P-I*'s editorial page. Besides the Nixon resignation, much had happened nationally and personally in those months. I had gained a creative, imaginative, and irreverent boss with whom I co-authored many editorials.

Sadly, that working relationship didn't last. The following year, we lost Ruth Howell to complications attributed to her aggressive Hodgkin's treatment. Following Ruth's sudden death in 1975, I applied for her job. It was a long shot; I had less than two years at the paper. But I had been encouraged by "Mother Cocker," who said that, although I likely wouldn't be considered, I had to apply or "not be taken seriously." It was excellent advice. I lost that position to John ("Jack") de Yonge, a more experienced colleague, but I did gain the title of assistant editorial page editor.

Dixy Lee Ray takes on a duck in this Ray Collins *Seattle Post-Intelligencer* editorial cartoon, circa 1978. *Ray Collins/SeattleP-I.com/Polaris.*

4

Dixy Takes on the
Big Boys, 1976–1980

The Watergate scandal and Richard Nixon's resignation left us with twin legacies: First, every mother's child dreamed of becoming a reporter like the *Washington Post*'s Bob Woodward and Carl Bernstein. Second, a disillusioned public wanted to vote for outsiders.

That anti-political mood affected the 1976 race for president, leading to the election of Georgia Gov. Jimmy Carter, a Democrat. A relative unknown on the national stage, he easily defeated then President Gerald Ford, an experienced GOP congressional leader. The public had an insatiable appetite for non-politicians. In the post-Watergate world, experience was not valued—it wasn't even a virtue.

The nation's anti-political mood also impacted state and local races that year. In Washington State, University of Washington professor and political novice Dixy Lee Ray was running for governor. She had chaired the U.S. Atomic Energy Commission and also served as director of Seattle's Pacific Science Center. Although important, those positions hardly substituted for governmental experience. Further, Dr. Ray's decision to run as a Democrat surprised many party veterans. Her views seemed more closely aligned with the Republican platform.

Even before taking office, Ray feuded with the press. During her campaign, she had a stock of horror stories about alleged political oversteps. She told about a certain southeast Washington business that supposedly was forced to close down over a trivial violation of the Clean Water Act. Its employees were said to be unemployed. When reporters asked about specifics, Ray grew defensive and refused to supply details.

However, *Seattle Post-Intelligencer* reporter Mike Layton finally pieced together the facts. He was able to reveal that her story was full of holes, essentially a right-wing myth meant to disparage safety regulations.

Despite her credentials as a marine biologist, Dr. Ray spoke against what she called "the environmental protectionist movement." She complained about rules and regulations that, she argued, "make it impossible to conduct a business."

Dr. Ray's unsupported charges, although well reported, didn't affect the public's thirst for supporting a newcomer. The voters apparently liked the idea of an outspoken woman candidate. They liked that she told it like it was—in her view. Her campaign ads read: "Little Lady Takes on the Big Boys." She made dozens of big promises, including reducing taxes and slashing state employment by 4,000 workers.

She aced the September 1976 primary election, besting Seattle Mayor Wes Uhlman and environmentalist Marvin Durning even in King County, their home territory. In the general election, she again did well, defeating King County Executive John Spellman, the Republican candidate. She took 53 percent of the vote, an amazing feat for a candidate new to elected office. Her campaign manager, the late Blair Butterworth, is famous for having said, "We thought she would be the best governor Washington ever had. Or the worst. And we were right." (Butterworth apparently opted for the latter. He did an about-face when Governor Ray sought a second term. Butterworth, a smooth operator irreverently called "Butterballs" by his friends and enemies, went to work on a campaign for Governor Ray's Democratic opponent, State Sen. Jim McDermott.)

After Dr. Ray's surprise election as the state's first woman governor, the *Post-Intelligencer* editorial staff—of which I was now a member—faced a coverage problem. Between the governor's political inexperience and her inability to censor her rhetoric, at least one critical editorial could have been written each day. For instance, there was the time when she sparked an international incident telling British Columbians to "mind your own business" over their opposition to a proposal to build an oil port near the Canadian border.

Then there was an ugly incident when her staff strong-armed Jerry Gay, a *Seattle Times* photographer. Governor Ray's staffers physically prevented Gay from taking the governor's picture while she was shaking hands with Len Sawyer, the discredited former Washington State House Speaker. There also was the occasion when she supported bringing supertankers into Puget Sound, and is said to have pooh-poohed environmental worries over a possible oil spill with the words: "Oh, you people go all gooey over ducks."

She enthusiastically supported atomic energy, having once referred to a nuclear warhead as "a beautiful piece of sculpture." She nixed a proposed cleanup at the Hanford, Washington, nuclear lab and even supported dumping nuclear waste into the ocean. It was a curious position for a marine biologist.

One of Ray's first actions as governor was to demand the resignation of all department heads, not an unusual tactic for a new governor. She also demanded the legislature return to her office 124 nominations for boards and commissions made by Gov. Dan Evans, her immediate predecessor. When asked about the massive firings, Ray dismissed the upcoming turmoil. She did offer to "send boxes of Kleenex along with the pink slips."

The governor's combative and sometimes outrageous tactics led Jack de Yonge, the *P-I*'s editorial page editor, to start daily editorial board meetings with a standard prayer: "For the health of Governor Ray." De Yonge reasoned it would keep the paper from being dragged into court for defamation and accused of showing "actual malice," a legal term that requires proof of ill will.

It didn't help that Ray refused to continue the regular Olympia press conferences initiated by former Governor Evans. Nor that she restricted press interviews to friendly reporters and even scheduled press opportunities in remote small towns she deemed pro-Dixy. She later added insult by naming a litter of piglets, born on her Fox Island farm, after her least favorite Olympia reporters. The *P-I*'s Mike Layton once said that naming a piglet in his honor was second in indignity to the time when Jacques, the governor's ever-present miniature poodle, relieved himself directly on Layton's foot.

The media often felt Governor Ray's wrath during her tumultuous four years as governor. Even prior to her inauguration, *P-I* columnist Shelby Scates and *Seattle Times* editorialist Don Hannula had been warned by the governor's aide Lou Guzzo, himself a former newsman, that they were about to learn "what the words *persona non grata* really mean."

On April 3, 1977, several months into Governor Ray's first year, Robert Harper, political reporter for the Olympia bureau of the Spokane *Spokesman-Review*, wrote: "Instead of honesty, openness and responsibility, the Ray administration has made itself the most inaccessible in 20 years in Olympia and has resorted to attacks on the press in place of straight-forward answers to policy questions. This policy reached the point last week where Governor Ray suggested that the Olympia press corps might be changed. She proposed that reporters be given limited terms because she said that even new reporters are too easily infected with the virus of cynicism."

I too was in the governor's doghouse, if not her pigpen. It was the result of my reporting on one of her infrequent Olympia press conferences. I wrote that she had added a few pounds during her tenure and described her as "chicly polyestered" in an ample peach-colored pantsuit. The significant news that reporters learned that day was Ray's flat contention that "A-bombs do not cause cancer." The governor had been welcoming radioactive waste to the Hanford Site in eastern Washington. In fact, 75 percent of the nation's military waste had already been stored there.

One of Dr. Ray's promises when she was running for governor was that she would reexamine the Department of Social and Health Services (DSHS). During her election campaign, she had termed the department "almost unmanageable." She was as good as her word. Even before she took office, she appointed a 15-member panel to recommend changes. In her first two years in office, she gave the department two task forces, four secretaries, three chiefs of corrections, three prison superintendents, and numerous other roster changes.

The *Post-Intelligencer* editorialized: "Citizens of the state, the DSHS professionals and the many poor and voiceless clients of the agency deserve better leadership." No question that Dr. Ray had called the department "almost unmanageable." Once elected, she had worked overtime to fulfill her prophecy.

Despite his *persona-non-grata* status, the *P-I*'s Shelby Scates managed to report that Governor Ray had been holding closed-door meetings with Chris Carlson, regional director for the U.S. Interior Department. Under discussion was Ray's ambitious plan to build an oil port in Puget Sound waters.

According to Scates' story, Carlson reminded the governor that Sen. Warren ("Maggie") Magnuson had expressly added an amendment to the 1977 Marine Mammal Protection Act forbidding oil port construction east of Port Angeles. What prompted Maggie's action was his response to Governor Ray's single-minded pursuit of a close-in oil port.

Carlson reported details of their meeting. He told Scates: "I pointed out to the governor that, as chairman of the Senate Appropriations Committee, Senator Magnuson had ample clout to stop the port."

Carlson said that Ray had looked daggers at him, clenched her jaw and then loudly proclaimed, "Warren Magnuson is not Jesus Christ!"

It was not the first or last time that Governor Ray and the all-powerful senator would cross swords. Among other divisive issues was a proposal that the state, in desperate need of more prison space, acquire the soon-to-close McNeil Island federal prison. State legislators favored such a transfer. They had even attached a rider to a state budget bill requiring the governor to act to acquire McNeil.

In response, Governor Ray repeatedly asserted that McNeil "would be best used for a wildlife sanctuary." Besides, she said, "Even if McNeil were available, which it is not, it would cost too much."

However, when contacted by the press—it was I (as a *P-I* editorial page staffer) who made the phone call—Senator Magnuson said he was not up to speed; he had not been briefed on McNeil Island. But he added, "If the state were to ask, I, of course, would try to be helpful." Good as his word, Magnuson later made sure the state was able to acquire the McNeil Island prison.

The spectacular natural disaster, the 1980 eruption of Mount St. Helens, occurred during Governor Ray's term in office. The mountain quaked and belched fumes in the weeks preceding its May 18 eruption. The volcano's awakening, marked by rumbling quakes, had prompted the governor to designate a red zone, a no-entry territory, around the mountain. Entry into the area was restricted by the governor's designation.

Afterward, with 57 lives lost, some thought that the no-entry zone should have encompassed a far larger, more evenly designated area. On the south side of the summit was a red zone, a 20-mile restricted area. On the north side, however, Governor Ray had drawn another line, a blue zone that restricted entry but allowed the Weyerhaeuser Company to continue logging within a mile of St. Helens' peak.

Many believed that Weyerhaeuser, one of Governor Ray's largest campaign supporters, had influenced the governor to draw the lopsided no-entry zones. The governor's possible bias did not go unnoticed by families and friends of individuals who died or were severely injured in the volcanic eruption. The massive explosion blew 1,300 feet from the mountain's summit, destroyed 250 homes, 47 bridges, and damaged 185 miles of roads and rail track.

How many of the 57 lost in the explosion and its nightmarish aftermath would have survived if the no-entry zone had covered a broader area? When questioned, the governor flatly assured reporters—and even convinced President Jimmy Carter—that the bulk of those who died had entered the red zone illegally.

A handful of injured survivors along with families of the deceased went to court, suing the state and Weyerhaeuser. King County Superior Court Judge James McCutcheon, who had been appointed to the bench by Governor Ray in the days after the May 18, 1980, eruption, promptly dismissed the state as a defendant. The judge ruled that the state was not responsible for deaths or injuries caused by the eruption.

Judge McCutcheon allowed the Weyerhaeuser suit to continue, but he limited the plaintiffs to Weyerhaeuser employees or their survivors. He also restricted dramatic testimony on the part of the severely injured. Finally, the judge gave jurors lengthy instructions, making it highly unlikely the plaintiffs could hope to recover much in the way of damages.

Was the governor influenced by Weyerhaeuser when she drew the unbalanced line? During a deposition, Governor Ray acknowledged that she had indeed talked to George Weyerhaeuser, the company's president. She admitted that she drew the line more narrowly on one side to give the timber company access to its lands. But she insisted that she did so only after Weyerhaeuser agreed to take full responsibility for "setting up a system of rapid warning." She added, "There was an understanding."

During his deposition, George Weyerhaeuser hedged, saying he "couldn't recall" talking to the governor about limiting the size of the restricted zone. Surprisingly, neither the governor nor the logging company president was called to testify during the trial. The outcome was a shockingly lowball settlement for the survivors and families. Once lawyers were paid, there was between $19,727 and $21,727 for each of the 11 plaintiffs. In all, the settlement cost the company only $240,000.

If the Mount St. Helens blast was the largest natural disaster of Governor Ray's term, the largest manmade disaster was the Taul Watanabe incident. Watanabe was one of the governor's biggest campaign supporters and closest political advisers. He had been linked to an alleged $23,500 bribe of former state Rep. Bob Perry and former state House Speaker Len Sawyer.

Perry, later convicted and sent to prison on federal charges, said the bribe aimed to promote interests of a large Japanese construction firm. That company, an ally of Watanabe's, was pushing for permission to build an oil port at Cherry Point in northern Puget Sound.

The governor herself confirmed that she had entrusted Watanabe to deal with state Senate Majority Leader Gordon Walgren over the issue. She convinced Watanabe to offer Walgren an appointment to the U.S. Senate seat should Warren Magnuson, her sometime foe, die in office. It may have been a cynical move on the governor's part because at the time Governor Ray knew that Walgren was under FBI investigation in connection with racketeering charges.

As the gubernatorial primary approached, Governor Ray went ballistic whenever asked about Taul Watanabe. She refused to answer questions from *P-I* reporters, forcing the paper to make arrangements to slip its questions to KOMO-TV reporters. Governor Ray brushed aside the *P-I*'s coverage, saying "it reflects on all Asian-Americans in our state." This seemed an extreme example of shooting the messenger and caused the *P-I* editorialist to ask, "Whatever happened to the Dixy Lee Ray who was elected as a non-politician promising to be forthright and candid?"

After four years steering the state erratically, Ray lost her bid for reelection in the 1980 September primary. She was soundly defeated by state Rep. Jim McDermott who had the support of Senator Magnuson. Also playing a large part in her defeat was strong opposition from environmental groups that Governor Ray had alienated during her volatile term. (In the 1980 general election, McDermott would lose the governor's race to Republican John Spellman.)

Ray may have sown the seeds for that extraordinary primary loss when she repeatedly sparred with the news media. It was the first denial of party backing for a seated governor's second term since 1908.

It is hard to win a fight with news media that can print negative stories like the one recounted by Pacific Science Center staffer Jim Anderson. He belatedly told reporters about Dr. Ray's infamous aggressive driving style. Anderson reported he had once ridden with her in a three-quarter-ton flatbed truck bound for the center. In her haste to park the oversized truck in the Pacific Science Center lot, she had "dented two cars, broken the taillight on a third and smashed a rear window on a fourth."

At the end of her single four-year term, Dr. Ray retired to her home on Fox Island. She and her former aide Lou Guzzo, once a top *Seattle P-I* editor, co-authored two books, *Trashing the Planet* in 1990 and *Environmental Overkill* in 1991. Her books were highly critical of the environmental movement and of climate change. She warned against drawing conclusions relying on scientific averages. To illustrate her point, she cited what would happen if you used averages in an attempt to define personhood: "The average person," said Ray, "would have one breast and one testicle." The governor never lacked a snappy quip.

Dr. Ray died on January 2, 1994. In a bizarre postscript, it was later discovered that individuals in the Pierce County medical examiner's office had unlawfully kept copies of her autopsy photos as macabre souvenirs. It was a grim ending to a colorful and combative career that few of us who were there at the time would ever forget.

5

"Seize that Vessel,"
1977–1989

After Washington voters elected Dixy Lee Ray, a nonpolitician, governor in the fall of 1976, the city of Seattle was getting ready to pick a candidate to replace two-term Mayor Wes Uhlman.

Mayor Uhlman, nicknamed "the white-maned wonder" (some suspected the youthful mayor, first elected in 1969 at the age of 34, dyed his locks to look more mature), was serving out his second term. He had already decided not to run for a third term. He may have been bruised by a string of troubles. A short list of woes included mayor–council infighting, anti-war demonstrations, race riots, aftermath of a police payoff scandal, and a bitter, although unsuccessful, recall attempt.

The Uhlman years (1970–78) were also marked by major transportation controversies. There was the push to build a vastly expanded Interstate-90 crossing of Lake Washington, shown in preliminary drawings as a 14-lane eyesore. The proposed surface design for I-90 all but obliterated the Mount Baker neighborhood.

Then there was contention over plans for a long-debated high-level West Seattle Bridge. The latter had already led to indictment of several prominent officials, including Democratic National Committeeman Luke Graham, Washington State Rep. Bob Perry, and Seattle City Engineer Robert Gulino. Mayor Uhlman had escaped the ugly West Seattle Bridge scandal with its charges of kickbacks and payoffs. But given the climate of governmental distrust, Uhlman could be excused for wanting to leave City Hall.

The field to replace the mayor was bewilderingly crowded. Fifteen contenders entered the primary, including four of the nine Seattle councilmembers: Phyllis Lamphere, Sam Smith, John Miller, and Wayne Larkin. There were two prominent outsiders, the director of the Seattle Department of Community Development, Paul Schell, and TV news analyst and commentator Charles Royer.

The crowded primary election ballot drew conflicting endorsements. None was more glowing than a rare solo recommendation for Phyllis Lamphere from *Post-Intelligencer* Publisher Bob Thompson. Thompson came to the *P-I* from Washington, DC, where he had covered presidents, congressmen, and Supreme Court justices. His was the long view. He wrote about Lamphere: "As president of the National League of Cities, she has national stature. As a lifelong local resident who has served 10 years on the City Council, she has an acute understanding of the problems this city faces. We have concluded that her name must lead all the rest."

The *P-I* endorsement of Lamphere was something of a sensation. The city had only once before elected a woman mayor, Bertha Knight Landes in 1926. Backing Lamphere was a move that many of us at the *P-I* heartily approved. I had written editorials about Lamphere's many accomplishments on the city council. She was renowned for sponsoring experimental traffic circles in neighborhoods, bringing greater safety to residential streets. She waged war on billboards, making progress removing some of the worst offenders. Her record of successes made the *P-I*'s backing a popular endorsement.

Endorsements aside, this still was an anti-government year. Not a single one of the councilmembers was able to survive the crowded primary election. Councilmember Lamphere had been attacked for being out of town too often during her year as president of the National League of Cities. She may also have been tarnished running as a woman at a time when the state's first woman governor, Dixy Lee Ray, was becoming notorious for her many eccentricities and stormy press relations.

In any case, two candidates new to electoral politics emerged from the Seattle primary. TV commentator Charles Royer and Community Development Director Paul Schell would face off in the general election. Schell, a lawyer who had moved to Seattle in 1967, had impeccable credentials as president of Allied Arts, the influential civic group that had campaigned successfully to save the Pike Place Market.

Of the two finalists, Royer was best known to the public. His face and pithy commentary aired nightly on KING-TV. As a relative newcomer (1970) to the area, Royer had been a dark horse entry into the race.

Like many a City Hall newsman before and since, Royer had taken stock of the lineup of candidates, some with slim credentials, and thought about running for mayor himself. Royer and fellow KING reporter Don McGaffin kicked around the crazy idea at Francisco's, a newsmen's bar on Dexter Avenue, as they readied for a joint 1977 year-end round-up appearance before the 30th District Democrats on Phinney Ridge.

When they got there, McGaffin, who still was carrying his unfinished Bloody Mary, brashly blurted out: "Ladies and gentlemen, let me introduce the man who, by the grace of God, will be your next mayor of Seattle." McGaffin was more prophetic than he knew.

Democrats in attendance erupted, cheering enthusiastically. Come January 1978 Royer was encouraged enough to quit his job as KING's news analyst, a move essential for any professional journalist, especially one charged with commenting on local politics. To help finance his campaign, Royer took out a second mortgage on his North End home. He formally declared his candidacy at a crowded event at the Serbian Hall in South Seattle.

The knock against Royer from the beginning was that he had virtually no governmental experience, save two years as PTA president of Nathan Eckstein Middle School. At the time, Royer's daughter Suzanne, a student at Eckstein, was living with Charley and his stately second wife, Russian and Middle European scholar Rosanne Gostovich Royer, in their View Ridge home.

Royer ran a grass-roots campaign, relying mainly on shoe leather, door-to-door contacts, and small donations. Since quitting his job at KING-TV, he had the time to create a base by attending neighborhood and Democratic district meetings. His campaign leaned heavily on family. Charley's younger brother Bob Royer, who had also worked at KING, and their mutual friend Dick Kelly ran operations. Rosanne, daughter of Serbo-Croatian immigrants, also helped out, making good use of her local connections.

In addition, Royer had the unacknowledged support of former colleagues in the KING-TV newsroom. Such backing was unethical for supposedly unbiased journalists. But, in fact, Royer's first support check, a $50 contribution, came from KING reporter Carol Lewis. KING-TV later assigned Lewis to cover the Schell campaign. Insiders at the time thought Lewis' coverage of Schell, Royer's opponent, was unduly harsh.

Royer's stump speech focused primarily on the public schools, on the need for school desegregation and on making Seattle "a better kids' place." His rhetoric sounded strangely misplaced. When he appeared before those of us on the *P-I* editorial board, he devoted the bulk of his time to talking about Seattle schools and less to other critical needs of the city.

After he left the meeting, we were all shaking our heads.

"What did he say he was running for? For mayor?" asked my boss, Jack de Yonge, the editorial page editor. "Could have sworn he wants to teach school."

Nevertheless, Royer scored points with Seattle voters for his outspoken support for the schools. He also tapped into the populist, anti-freeway mood and opposition to a massive Interstate-90 expansion.

Royer spotlighted his anti-growth stance, whereas his opponent Paul Schell, as the city's director of community development, was more open to increased density. The two clashed repeatedly over development of the Westlake Mall. Royer criticized the grandiose plan developed by Mayor Uhlman and the city council, favoring a plan that would move the Seattle Art Museum to Westlake Mall. Meanwhile, Schell proposed a major Westlake redevelopment that would include two new public squares, theaters, and a hotel.

In the end, after countless one-on-one debates, Royer beat Schell easily. Royer had made good use of his on-air presence and his knack for appealing to an audience. One positive attribute was his ability to make politics seem like fun. Even avowed opponents like David Brewster, *Seattle Weekly* editor/publisher, conceded that "only Royer's campaign has any feeling of energy and freshness."

If "campaigning as fun" was Charley's strength, governing came off as less-than-fun, fraught with errors and false starts. One of Royer's initial problems was fitting in at City Hall. He had, after all, run the primary race against several sitting councilmembers. Another obstacle was his decision to hire his two campaign managers, his brother Bob and Dick Kelly, as deputy mayors. Neither had any more governing experience than did Charley.

The city's daily newspapers, both *Times* and *P-I*, didn't hesitate to pick on the wobbly new administration. They were bitingly sarcastic over Royer's selection of his younger brother as deputy mayor. At the *P-I*, Jack de Yonge mocked the choice during the editorial board's morning meetings. As assistant editorial page editor, I attended these meetings and recall de Yonge dismissively referring to "Deputy Bob." At other times, he took to identifying the Royer brothers as "CharleyBob."

Ironically, the former newsman and commentator initially had difficulty dealing with the media. Royer started out trying to make everything available to the press, but quickly found out that making executive decisions required a certain amount of discretion.

Soon after taking office, Royer instituted twice-weekly backgrounders with the press. But to keep things informal, he ruled that TV cameras would not be allowed. It was a rookie mistake. Royer quickly realized his error when new KING reporter Linda Brill crashed the mayor's office with TV cameras rolling.

Brill caught Royer aide Carol Lewis, the former KING-TV reporter, in a failed attempt to block the cameras. The story of former journalists trying to limit coverage even made the pages of the *New York Times*.

Too often, Royer overreacted to less than admiring reports. Early in his first term, he apparently grew so weary of the *Post-Intelligencer's* negativity that he called then *P-I* City Hall reporter Tim Egan into his office. According to Egan's report, Charley and Bob closed the office door and double-teamed him, giving him a verbal scalding for what they saw as unfair reporting.

Never having the benefit of management experience (his single credential was a brief stint as a Sears management trainee in the late 1950s), Royer had lessons to learn. He himself later admitted that some early appointments were less than stellar.

One of his first important decisions was picking new leadership at Seattle City Light. Both Royer and campaign opponent Paul Schell had promised that, if elected, they would fire controversial City Light Superintendent Gordon Vickery. A former fire chief, Vickery had stirred militant opposition to reforms at the municipal utility. Vickery's management style even prompted an 11-day wildcat strike.

Despite his campaign promises to fire Vickery, the new mayor discovered to his dismay that he couldn't legally take action until the superintendent's contract expired. When Vickery conveniently left to take a federal job in 1978, Royer took the opportunity to nominate Robert Murray, an Oregon energy consultant.

However, Royer failed to get a buy-in from City Councilmember Randy Revelle, who headed the council's Energy Committee and who had his own views and a good understanding of City Light issues. Revelle responded by holding up the confirmation through four stormy months of discussion, punctuated with 36 hours of contentious public hearings. Eventually Murray squeaked by, winning confirmation with a 5–4 city council vote. Revelle voted with the opposition.

Law enforcement also presented a problem. Former Mayor Wes Uhlman had earlier hired George Tielsch, a tough, military-minded Californian, to clean up the scandal-ridden Seattle Police Department. As chief, the hard-nosed Tielsch was mostly successful at internal house cleaning, but he ended up tolerating continued collection of secret police files on hundreds of Seattleites.

Later it was discovered that the city's police had been keeping track of community leaders such as Charley Royer and his colleague Don McGaffin. Police spying had gotten out of hand, collecting information on hundreds of citizens not involved in the commission of crimes. Board members of the Seattle League of Women Voters, for example, came under police surveillance for having ordered copies of Mao Zedong's "Little Red Book" for study sessions on China.

In 1974 when Tielsch resigned and left Seattle to return to his native California, Uhlman appointed Robert Hanson, an internal hire, as chief of police. Hanson looked and acted the part of the tough Irish cop. At a meeting in the *P-I's* third-floor conference room, Chief Hanson met with those of us serving on the editorial page. He was responding to our heated questions about the secret police files when he suddenly stopped speaking. Hanson paused and looked out the conference room window at the Grosvenor House, an apartment complex directly across Wall Street.

"Don't know why you guys are steamed up over a lousy bunch of police files when you're sitting across the street from the city's largest whore house," said Hanson. It was an irrelevant remark and probably not defensible. But what came next was even more astonishing. Hanson said, "Besides, just so you know, I destroyed 700 of those dang files yesterday."

Discovery of the files had been one step toward ending widespread police spying initially brought on by anti-war and racial violence within the city. Police officers like Seattle Police Major Ray Connery had defended spying. He told the city council that Seattle was "the bombing capital of the United States." He claimed, "Seattle had more bombs going off per capita in the city than anywhere else in the country."

City Councilmember Michael Hildt responded to Connery saying, "I don't want to be bombed either, but I don't think we have to face the choice between being bombed and having intelligence activity that is not justified on the basis of reasonable grounds of evidence."

Outrage over the department's out-of-control spy network finally led to passage of a city ordinance. The law restricted police to gathering only information relevant to criminal investigations. It was something Mayor Royer, himself a target of overzealous intelligence gathering, heartily approved and quickly signed into law.

In the wake of the file fracas Chief Hanson resigned in 1978, leaving H. A. Vanden Wyer to serve an interim stint as chief. After a nationwide search, Mayor Royer appointed New York Assistant Chief Patrick Fitzsimons to head the force. The story of Fitzsimons' introduction to the city would become the stuff of legend.

As Fitzsimons told the story, he and his wife Olga were staying at the Olympic Hotel during interviews for the chief's job. Unable to sleep at 2 a.m. on a rainy Sunday, Fitzsimons called his wife to the hotel window. As they watched, they saw a street deserted of vehicles, but there were pedestrians standing on the rain-whipped corner, patiently waiting for the "walk" light.

Impressed with the law-abiding display, Fitzsimons turned to Olga and made a snap decision to accept the job if it were offered. He said, "We're staying here."

Chief Fitzsimons took the job and quickly gained respect from the force. One cop recalled how he often saw the chief at precinct role calls. Fitzsimons would personally pound on officers' chests, checking to see if they were wearing their protective vests. Although sometimes criticized by city councilmembers for failure to relate better to minority communities and for his inability to hire more minorities and women, Fitzsimons stayed for a record 15 years. Royer would later count Fitzsimons as one of his best appointments.

Mayor Royer was famous, if not infamous, for the numbers of comely young women he appointed to management positions. City Hall observers thought some of Royer's appointments owed more to appearance than to skill. City Hall, some said, was beginning to look "more like a dating bureau than an urban government."

One early hire, to no one's surprise, was Carol Lewis, the stunningly attractive KING reporter, his first campaign donor. He hired her as a special mayoral assistant, but then nominated her to be temporary head of the city's Office of Policy Planning (OPP). The appointment was seen as an affront to the city council. Councilmembers had heeded the mayor's plea not to kill the policy planning office outright, but to wait for his planned reorganization.

Who had lobbied the council to save OPP? Carol Lewis. On several levels, her nomination flew in the face of a recent directive on how to fill city jobs. The council had voted on a process that required searching for the most qualified candidate and also looking for minority candidates. Still Lewis did manage to get the temporary job and later would serve a stint as deputy mayor before taking over management of the Seattle Center.

During Royer's first year, he fielded much adverse press, including damaging accounts of an August lawn-party picnic that got out of hand. Royer buddy Don McGaffin organized the alfresco soiree, sited near the historic columns on the University of Washington campus. Since the picnic date happened to fall on the anniversary of the first shots fired in World War I, guests arrived wearing period costumes: tuxedoes and high-waisted gowns. They dined elegantly on game hen, May wine, and sugared strawberries served on fine china,

As the evening wore on, the party-goers, allegedly hyped on various mood-altering substances, grew rowdy enough to prompt repeated visits from the UW campus police. Subsequently, the *P-I*'s Emmett

Watson wrote a column accusing the Royer circle of elitism. The pugnacious McGaffin responded, threatening to punch both Watson and the *P-I* city editor in the nose. Later, he backed off, unwilling to take on a medium with half a million readers.

Not forgotten by those readers was the fact that a promised high-level West Seattle Bridge—a replacement for the Spokane Street bridge—had been hotly debated during the Royer-Schell mayoral campaign. When pressured about the new bridge, estimated to cost more than $100 million, Royer had answered that the city lacked the money.

As a city thoroughfare, not a state or federal route, there were no funds available beyond a few million from an earlier bond issue backed by Forward Thrust, a civic improvement movement. When appealed to for help, the federal highway administrator flatly told the *Seattle Times* that federal funds were a non-starter. The administrator added, jokingly: "Short of a tug knocking the bridge out."

The freighter *Antonio Chavez* that hit the West Seattle Bridge made the *Seattle Post-Intelligencer*'s editorial page "Newsmaker of the Month" on July 3, 1978, in this Bob McCausland cartoon. *SeattleP-I.com/Polaris.*

And that, miraculously, was close to what happened. At 2:38 a.m. on June 11, 1978, the *Antonio Chavez*, a Greek freighter, guided by an 80-year-old Puget Sound pilot, Rolf Neslund, struck the Spokane Street Bridge, locking the north span into an open position. The damaged low-level bascule bridge seemed to be giving the city "the bird."

Amidst the resulting confusion, the bridge tender mistakenly phoned former mayor Wes Uhlman, who hollered into the phone: "Call the goddamned mayor, will you?"

By the time Mayor Royer received the bridge tender's call, all he could think to say was: "Seize the vessel!"

The next day city officials soberly assessed the traffic-confounding problem. They figured they could count on help from Seattle's Brock Adams, then Secretary of Transportation, and also on rock-solid Sen. Warren Magnuson, still chair of Appropriations and known for his "little amendments" (measures he slipped into routine spending bills).

At the city level, Councilmember Jeanette Williams, who was determined to deliver a high-level bridge to West Seattle, called in funds from the state, the Port of Seattle, and King County. The high-level bridge that soared above the Duwamish Waterway was under construction by 1981 and finished in 1984, during Mayor Royer's second term. Later it would be renamed the "Jeanette Williams Memorial Bridge."

A macabre postscript to the Chavez story was the fate of the marine pilot, Rolf Neslund, who subsequently disappeared. His wife Ruth claimed he had returned to his native Norway. Investigators later discovered that he and Ruth, a bed-and-breakfast owner on Lopez Island, had quarreled drunkenly over Rolf's pension money. Ruth shot her husband twice and with help from her brother chopped and incinerated the body, burying the ashes in a compost pile. Ruth eventually was convicted. She served the remainder of her life in prison, writing frequent letters to those of us on the *P-I* editorial page. She complained about conditions at Purdy, the women's prison in Gig Harbor, and detailed instances of what she saw as mistreatment.

Meanwhile, construction of the high-level West Seattle Bridge and resolution of the Westlake Mall redevelopment could be counted among Royer's increasing successes. When the Seattle Art Museum declined to relocate at Westlake, Mayor Royer was able to enlist a new private partner, the Rouse Company, to manage a four-story retail mall, backed by a 25-story office tower. The city enhanced the public plaza to the south with decorative paving, a monumental arch, and a cascading water feature.

The water feature's design originally included a million-dollar misting machine. Who could have imagined that foggy Seattle needed manufactured mist? The machine frankly was a one-minute wonder. When first turned on, the mist cloud enveloped and obscured traffic on Fourth Avenue. It was an interesting idea, but the mister had to be sacrificed to serious safety concerns.

Royer had enjoyed modest success taming I-90. Instead of the proposed 14-lane speedway, he whittled the route down to a configuration dubbed "3-2T-3"—three vehicle lanes in each direction and two transit lanes. Another success was the decision to partially lid the freeway's destructive entry into the city, averting the planned destruction of the Mount Baker neighborhood.

The one-term-and-learning mayor had little trouble with re-election in 1981, easily besting Sam Smith, Seattle's first African American councilmember. Smith's staggered term allowed him to retain his council seat while running for mayor and at the same time keeping his name in front of the voters. Smith's campaign gave him free swipes at the mayor over his frequent out-of-town travel, a paradox since Royer, when working as a KING-TV commentator, had attacked Mayor Uhlman for just such trips. Smith also targeted Deputy Mayor Bob Royer, focusing on what Smith saw as Bob's unstatesmanlike behavior.

In one such instance, Bob had complained at the Washington Public Power Supply System (WPPSS) board meeting that the system's overinflated budget could buy "three billion Tootsie Rolls or 300 pounds of marijuana." Bob, who filled in when Charley was out of town, became notorious for his forthright but uncensored correspondence. He was not above lecturing reporters, publishers, and even city councilmembers.

Once Charley Royer became involved with other elected mayors on the national scene, the Seattle mayor discovered a taste for new challenges. He became involved in the National League of Cities, winning election as its president. His byline appeared in national publications including the *Washington Post*. His name began surfacing for higher office.

When Sen. Henry ("Scoop") Jackson died unexpectedly September 1, 1983, Gov. John Spellman appointed former Gov. Dan Evans to fill the seat until a November special election. Charley was among the hopefuls who filed for the Senate seat. Forced into a statewide campaign, he stumbled, coming in a dismal fourth behind Evans, Congressman Mike Lowry, and Lloyd Cooney, a conservative broadcasting executive. At a minimum, Charley's lackluster run served to focus his attention back on the city and its acute needs.

In the meantime, Bob Royer distinguished himself with one of the signal achievements of CharleyBob's second term. Bob was instrumental in resolving a decade-long controversy over the plan to raise Seattle City Light's Ross Dam on the Skagit River. The plan would have completely flooded a Canadian valley. In exchange for Seattle abandoning the plan, British Columbia agreed to supply an equivalent amount of electric power to the city.

Charley subsequently won an unprecedented third term defeating a challenge from Councilmember Norm Rice. In all, he served 12 full years, becoming the city's only mayor to date to serve three consecutive four-year terms. However, many observers would feel that Charley's final term had been the least productive, a headache-filled stretch marked by continued squabbles over environmental and regional issues.

For one, there was the problem of garbage. The city's landfills in Kent and Midway had drawn increased opposition from suburban officials and residents. Those landfills also prompted a lawsuit filed by the state.

What to do with the city's thousands of daily truckloads of trash? Charley proposed a garbage incinerator. Where such an incinerator would be sited and how it would affect the environment were troublesome issues. During the controversy, Greenpeace board member Shelley Stewart committed a green-collar crime. She stole the garbage can from the Royer home and put the contents on public display at a meeting called to discuss incinerator plans.

The Royers, hosts at a house party that week, had disposed of many items of trash—paper plates and plastic cups—that should have been properly recycled under the city's new solid waste code. Shelley's theft was a golden opportunity, an invitation to satire. By then, I had transitioned to a new job at the *P-I* and was writing a four-day-a-week city column. Naturally, I had carte blanche to speculate on possible contents of the Royers' trash. My own list of imagined items included a bottle filled with sand and seaweed, and a note that read: "Help. Save me. Marooned on a desert island, Brother Bob."

Charley's relatives, Bob among them, qualified as public figures and were considered fair game by the news media. Bob got into print over the 1982 Seattle Ethics and Elections probe of a no-bid contract awarded to his then wife, cultural anthropologist and relationship counselor Jennifer James. Dr. James had received $600 for a three-hour lecture to City Water Department personnel on "interpersonal issues between men and women in the workplace." Bob claimed no knowledge of the contract, but because Washington is a community property state, Bob clearly stood to profit and was fined over the contract.

Later Bob and Jennifer again made the news when they called it quits and filed for divorce. Confirmation of the rumored split became a contest between the two Seattle daily newspapers. When phoned, Jennifer James refused to comment to *Times* columnist Alf Collins. Bob, however, gave an affirmative response when I called. It was, as I pointed out, better to have the story made public, rather than having to explain one-on-one to friends and acquaintances.

Similarly, relations between Charley and Rosanne apparently were not always smooth. As Charley's third term wound down, it was announced that he would become director of the Institute of Politics at Harvard's John F. Kennedy School of Government.

"Goodbye Charley" events filled the calendar. He was called "beloved" and "Seattle's urban mayor of the year," among other accolades. However, one downtown luncheon event featured a roast with acid remarks that caused guests to ask one another, "Was that just a joke or was it for real?"

Rosanne Royer gave the mayor a surprisingly bittersweet send-off. When her turn to speak came, she said she would accompany her husband back East, but "only because, you know, Charley, you're my ticket to Boston." Did she mean to be so dismissive? We were never sure. But in 1992, three years later, the Royers split. All records of their divorce were sealed by a King County Superior Court judge.

Personal matters aside, Royer's 12 years as mayor held much to admire. During his three terms in office, he opened 20 community clinics around the city and with help from Senator Magnuson wrested control of the Public Health Hospital on Beacon Hill from federal hands. Charley became identified with public housing for low-income and senior residents, having promoted successful bond issues in 1981 and 1986 and, as a result, Seattle was delivering more low-income units than the entire state of California.

Seattle prospered during Royer's tenure, despite its increasing big-city problems: traffic, homelessness, and white flight from the schools. Royer had much success working to turn Seattle into a "kid's place," providing incentives for young people to stay in school and offering transit benefits. During his leadership, Seattle was named the nation's most livable city and Royer one of the 20 best big city mayors.

6

Saving the Market
Once Again, 1989–1991

The Pike Place Public Market, this city's heart of hearts, has been threatened and saved almost as many times as Pauline, the silent movie heroine who was tied to railroad tracks, thrown into the raging river, and left hanging on a cliff before her miraculous rescue.

The Market was born in 1907 when the skyrocketing price of onions ($1 a pound in the days of five-cent coffee) drove penny-wise shoppers to circumvent middlemen and start buying directly from farmers. Local growers trucked produce from their South Seattle farms and parked on Pike Place. Over the next decades, the Public Market evolved into a long arcade of street stalls and a collection of multi-level buildings perched on the steep bluff above the waterfront.

Public Market Center sign at sunset, Pike Place Market, June 2000. *Seattle Municipal Archives, Item 103795*

By the late 1960s, the Market was a thriving if rundown city fixture. That's when ambitious developers, backed by the city's Central Association, hatched a plan to redevelop the choice cliffside real estate. They wanted to demolish the Market, build an office complex, a luxury hotel, 5,000-car parking garage, and for nostalgia buffs, a pared-down replica of the old Market. In the developers' plan, the Market itself would be reduced to a couple of food stalls.

The story of how the Pike Place Public Market was saved from would-be urban renewal—some called it "urban removal"—is legendary. It stars Victor Steinbrueck, a University of Washington architecture professor, and a rag-tag crew of activists, academics, and artists known as the "Friends of the Market."

The Market's rescuers also included pro bono lawyers like Jerry Thonn who authored Referendum 71 and helped obtain the signatures needed to put preservation before Seattle voters.

Referendum 71 drew immediate opposition from those eager to redevelop the Market property. Opponents included downtown businesses, both daily newspapers, and many city officials. But the developers hadn't figured on Professor Steinbrueck and the Friends. Despite the lopsided odds, they rallied people to fight against the ravage of renewal. When the referendum reached the ballot in 1971, more than 70 percent voted to preserve their beloved Pike Place Public Market.

The Market was saved in 1971, complete with a historical commission to maintain the seven-acre district, a constituency group for market buffs, and a public development authority to oversee the precious real estate.

While Seattle residents and visitors have often heard that story, what isn't as often recounted was the tale of how the Market had to be rescued once again in the 1990s, some 20 years later. The Market was saved for the second time through the leadership of City Councilmember Peter Steinbrueck, son of the late Victor Steinbrueck, along with another group of allies, the Citizens Alliance to Save the Market.

The second rescue involved a fierce two-year battle over legal ownership of the 11 historic buildings that make up the Pike Place Market. Although the 1971 referendum rescued the Market from a city government itching to bulldoze it, the Market's thorny financial problems remained.

Where would the money come from to repave the Market? Repair the leaks? Prop up the aging buildings? At first Uncle Sam's money helped, thanks mainly to federal grants, $50 million in all, channeled to the Market by the late U.S. Senator Warren Magnuson. Federal money was used to renovate and to acquire the seven-acre Market and its buildings.

But Magnuson, the Market's longtime benefactor, lost his reelection in 1980 and with rents unable to keep pace the Market needed yet another infusion of cash. Finally in the mid-1980s, the Preservation and Development Authority came up with what looked like a grand scheme. The PDA planned to "sell" the Market buildings—a paper sale only—to a private investor who could pay millions towards needed improvements while taking advantage of federal preservation tax credits. The PDA, as an arm of the city, couldn't take advantage of those tax credits, but under federal law a private firm could. It looked like free money.

Three Market buildings were sold in 1981 to a New York investment firm, the Urban Holding Corporation, a group composed of five limited partnerships. In 1984 another eight buildings were sold to the Urban Group.

How in the world could they sell the Market, the defining landmark of the city? At the time PDA Director John Clise and his staff were certain they had found a foolproof scheme.

As explained to the PDA Board, the deal would provide adequate safeguards for all parties. The Market would get the millions it so desperately needed; the investors would get lucrative tax advantages, and the PDA would continue to manage the Market. In other words: business as usual. At the end of 20 years, a balloon payment written into the contract supposedly guaranteed that the investors would walk away.

The deal appeared fail-safe. Besides, they chorused: "Everyone's doing it." And, in fact, the Urban Group had already invested in Tacoma's historic Pantages Theatre, the Broadway Market, and the New Central Hotel in the International District.

During the early 1980s, there were many such deals around the country. Conversely, there were similar transactions that failed to take place—fortunately, as it turned out. The Metropolitan Tract, the University of Washington's lucrative downtown holdings, dodged a "tax sale" when questions arose over the legal arrangements. Attorney Gordon Culp, then a university regent, commented, "We couldn't see that there was much value."

Attitudes at the Market lacked such healthy skepticism. The tax sale looked like unearthing a pot of gold. Precautions would be taken. Loopholes plugged. Lawyers churned out a phonebook-sized stack of documents. All seemed well.

That is until the drama's next act. The federal government changed tax shelter laws in 1986: No more historic preservation credits. Meanwhile, the investors who had contributed some $3 million showed up to take charge. They arrived in person in December 1989, staying in downtown hotels at Market expense. They were dead certain they had bought the Market and they weren't satisfied with the way the PDA was managing it.

Arthur Malman, head of the Urban Group, said, "What we want is for the PDA to live up to documents they signed and recognize that we are entitled to a fair return on our investments." The Urban Group hired Arthur Anderson, the giant accounting firm, to do a "hostile" audit of Market finances and review the last eight years of operations. Adding to their attack arsenal, Malman hired Bob Gogerty, partner in Gogerty & Stark, a prominent Seattle-based public relations firm, to represent the Urban Group.

Although prospects looked grim, Peter Steinbrueck started alerting people. As a city columnist at the *Post-Intelligencer*, I was one of the first to hear the news. I spent hours on the phone with Peter, who worried that if the hostile audit found irregularities the PDA would be forced either to reimburse the investors or face termination of its management agreement.

Peter was clear: Should there be any abnormalities—something anyone who knew the Market could imagine—then someone else, maybe a New York company, would end up running the Market. The rumor mill buzzed with doomsday reports that, in any case, the absentee landlords had plans to triple rents charged to Market tenants.

In a November 30, 1989, *P-I* column, I wrote about the Market's predicament, concluding, "The Pike Place Public Market, the essence of Seattle, is in peril. At best, the Market managers are facing some difficult possibly unpleasant negotiations with New York investors at a December summit meeting. At worst the Market may be in danger of becoming; alas, may already have become the Pike Place Private Market."

My column was the first newspaper story to report on the Market's plight, a scoop that I would have preferred never to have written. The implications were frightening to anyone who loved the Market and especially to someone like me, who considered it "my beat." Seldom was the week when I didn't have a story or two about events at the Market.

The battle got underway with Urban Group President Arthur Malman and Martin Major, its vice president, arranging for a series of meetings to quiet fears. The two New Yorkers had been schooled in advance on the Seattle look. Malman arrived for the *P-I* session with a disarming smile. He was wearing not a business suit but a cable knit fisherman's sweater. He tried to sell himself as a Market booster.

The meeting, one of several I attended, featured Malman and Major spreading manufactured charm. But 100-watt grins aside, the pair were all business. Malman was cuttingly clear on a number of fronts. He insisted that, from the beginning, the Urban Group was interested in owning the Market rather than reaping short-term tax benefits. He declared, "We always buy. We never sell."

Malman claimed Market expenses had run wild, showing a 120 percent increase from 1983 to 1987. Further, he said the PDA hadn't provided the Urban Group with sufficient supporting data on expenses. As an example of excesses, he cited the Market's pending lease for the Pike Place Child Care Center, which he found "unacceptable." He said the lease was for a large segment of "our space," for more than three years and "substantially below its market value."

Malman wrote PDA Director Mike Carroll a chilling letter, saying, "You leave us no choice but to consider implementing far-reaching changes to management."

Relationships grew even icier. In December 1989 Malman learned to his dismay that each time he wrote to PDA director Carroll, his letter, often scrawled with editorial comments, was quickly released to the media and to tenants and friends of the Market. Although Malman complained bitterly, the PDA's deputy director John Turnbull responded saying, "We don't divulge employee records and sales data, but, as a public agency, we assume that our files are open to the public."

In January 1990 Malman's PR consultant Bob Gogerty issued a broadside. He blamed "provincialism" and "New York bashing" for the public's negative response to the Urban Group. Spokesman Gogerty said, "This idea that these are 'New York investors' instead of 'investors in the Market' is unhealthy. I had hoped people would look at them as they are. They do have a legal hold on the Market."

The public's reaction—similar to discovering a family of skunks in one's kitchen—was not surprising. People were incensed when they become aware of the Urban Group's strong-armed tactics and legal stranglehold over the Market. Represented as a mere "paper sale," it was reported that the highly opportunistic Urban Group had already realized $10 million in tax credits on a slightly less than $3 million investment. Further, the Urban Holding Group—sometimes known to angry Seattleites as UHG (pronounced "Ugh!")—had just released a new prospectus that revealed a plan to triple Market rents over a dozen years, confirming those scary early rumors.

This time, unlike the first Pike Place rescue when both the *P-I* and *Times* backed the plan to demolish the Market, both papers strongly editorialized against the Urban Group's high-handed takeover plans.

Gogerty, the Urban Group spokesman, confirmed he was quitting an advisory committee, appointed by then Mayor Norm Rice to work out differences. Gogerty said, "I thought we could sit down and settle this. Now I am not so sure we can get a fair trial in the court of public opinion." Also resigning the committee was another Urban Group representative, attorney Irwin Treiger. Gogerty's parting comment: "Maybe we'll have to go to court."

That indeed was where the case was headed. All sides were lawyering up. Peter Steinbrueck assembled a high-powered team of local lawyers who volunteered their time, pro bono, on behalf of the Citizens Alliance. The legal team, helped along again by attorney Jerry Thonn, concluded that State Constitution Article 8, section 7, with its prohibition against lending the state's credit, would void the sale and rescue the Market.

Steinbrueck also convinced Seattle City Attorney Mark Sidran to throw support from the city's legal team into the effort to keep the Market public. The PDA hired its own lawyers, including Gerald ("Gerry") Johnson, Sen. Magnuson's former chief of staff. It was Johnson who advised the PDA staff that a tough negotiator was needed. They got one: Shelly Yapp, former deputy mayor under Charley Royer.

By spring 1990, an array of lawsuits and counter suits erupted between the four involved parties. The cases ended up in Superior Court Judge Frank L. Sullivan's courtroom and the Market supporters won the first round.

The court of public opinion was also siding with the Market. Say what you like about Seattle, but where else would legal hassles be set to folk music? A catchy theme song, "The Pike Place Market Rag," was written by attorney William B. Knowles and sung to the tune of "The M.T.A.," made famous by the Kingston Trio. The "Rag" begins:

> Let me tell you the story 'bout the Pike Place Market
> And its sad condition today.
> In 1971 it was bought by the people
> And entrusted to the PDA.
> Well now, people of Seattle, don't you think it's a scandal
> That they gave our Market away?....

Final verse and chorus:

> So now, people of Seattle, if you're tired of this scandal,
> Well there's just one thing to say,
> Read the state constitution: Article 8, section 7,
> And just refuse to pay.
> Stop the rent increases, oust the Urban Group,
> Put the Public back in the PDA.

Public outcry to the contrary, the Urban Group was not giving up without a fight. The principals responded with a clever tactic, filing bankruptcy in federal court in New York. That placed Judge Frank Sullivan's favorable-to-the-city ruling (and the pending legal fees) on hold. It also moved the battle to New York where—said conventional wisdom—it would be far easier for Urban to prevail.

Once again, the Market had to rely on champions. PDA attorney Fred Tausend and Seattle City Attorney Mark Sidran, rather than just cite the law, argued the value of the Market's history, showing pictures, and calling it "the soul of Seattle." The New York judge bought their argument and sent the case back to Seattle Bankruptcy Court and Superior Judge Frank Howard.

Legal battles raged over many months. But in May 1991, when Judge Howard ruled that Judge Sullivan's order could be enforced against the Urban Group, the investors appeared ready to settle and give up all interest in the Market in return for cash to invest elsewhere. Thanks were due in large part to negotiator Shelly Yapp who got the PDA to agree to a buyout.

Many citizens, however, were still appalled at the idea of having to pay off the New Yorkers. Others heaped blame on the PDA for having "sold" the Market in the first place.

One underlying reason for the settlement was that all parties were hemorrhaging money. In an article in *Washington Law* magazine, the rhetorical question asked was: "How did a legal battle over a $2.93 million investment escalate into a combined legal bill of $4 million?"

The PDA had all but depleted its reserve fund, despite many pro bono donations. Meanwhile, the Urban Group owed $150,000 to a bankruptcy attorney, a local who probably would be out of pocket. Biggest loser of all was the Urban Group's original law firm, Bogle & Gates, which may have lost as much as $600,000. The lawsuits gave rise to the term "Bogle-izing." It came to mean "generating excessive paperwork." *Washington Law* magazine quoted Assistant City Attorney Randy Gainer as saying the suits generated "over a million documents."

Are there that many file drawers anywhere? Gainer claimed he was misquoted. He later corrected the quote: "A million pages, maybe. But a million documents, no."

In the aftermath, the Citizens Alliance, the City of Seattle, and the PDA jointly lobbied the state legislature for money to fund a settlement. The state came up with a $1.5 million appropriation. The city authorized $750,000 and the title companies matched that, giving the Urban Group a $3 million buyout. Settlement was reached in July 1991, with the final details worked out in October 1991. The good news: the city had rescued the Pike Place Public Market for a second time.

"The Pike Place Market Rag" had envisioned just the right steps: "Stop the rent increases, oust the Urban Group, and put the public back in PDA." With all that accomplished, Seattle could breathe easier. Once again the city managed to save its soul.

Mayor Rice speaking at the Public Safety Building Plaza in honor
of slain law enforcement officers, May 1990. *Seattle Municipal
Archives, Item 77399*

7

Mayor Nice to the Rescue, 1989–1998

It was the last Friday in July 1989, the final day of filing to run for mayor of Seattle, and a dozen contenders had already filed. They were prepping to win the office that Charley Royer was leaving after a record 12 years, three terms in all.

As the clocked ticked down on July 28, a lone applicant showed up at King County's elections office. City Councilmember Norman Blann Rice approached the window and paid his fee to enter the mayor's race. He made the deadline with just 20 minutes to spare.

Seattle politicos thereafter referred to an eleventh-hour filing as "doing a Norm."

Rice's entry into the race came as a total surprise, particularly shocking since he had loudly and repeatedly declared that, no, he would NOT run. In fact, he had been there, done that before without success. In 1985, four years previously, he had entered the race for mayor, but had been beaten soundly by incumbent Charles Royer.

What was the reason for Rice's sudden about face? Some suspected that, despite his position as a strong contender, he had deliberately delayed, waiting until the last minute, counting on the surprise element to make his candidacy newsworthy.

Rice had an alternative explanation. He said his mind was changed by the ugly debate over the "Save Our Schools" (SOS) anti-busing initiative. He told his supporters he had hoped some of the announced candidates would offer leadership to heal divisions within the city. He said he hadn't heard from anyone who would champion that vision.

Rice's speech explaining his late entry was one of his finest moments.

He said: "In the time since I declined to offer myself as a candidate for mayor, a terrible new ingredient has been added: the so-called SOS initiative to segregate our schools. While I applaud candidates, who have stood up against this initiative, you must know I cannot stand on the sidelines. I must join this battle with all my soul and resources. I believe the election of Seattle's next mayor offers the best and most powerful arena for pressing the battle against division and for unity."

Rice insisted he'd come to the decision to run only in the waning hours and without the benefit of opinion polls, paid consultants, or a healthy war chest. That his change of heart was totally last minute, not planned, was confirmed by his closest advisers, among them public affairs consultant Bob Gogerty, state Democratic Party Chair Charles Rolland, and historian Walt Crowley. Was Rice's last-minute entry a clever ploy or was it honest emotion? Before running for council and for the mayor's office, Rice had made a habit of first soliciting advice from opinion leaders. On several occasions, he invited me (at the time a *Post-Intelligencer* columnist) to talk about his prospects over coffee. Our friendship went back several years. We had known one another as fellow students, contemporaries at the University of Washington School of Communications in the early 1970s.

A Denver native, Rice had capped his communications degree with a Master of Public Administration degree from the UW Evans School of Public Affairs. He earned the degree while working at KOMO and KIXI radio and serving as assistant director at the Seattle Urban League. He later married Dr. Constance Williams, owner of a small public relations business, and took a corporate communications position with Rainier National Bank.

It would only be a matter of time before Rice parlayed his broad and varied background into electoral politics. In 1978, after Councilmember Phyllis Lamphere resigned to accept a job as regional director of the Economic Development Administration, Rice won the special election to fill her council seat. He was reelected in 1983 and 1987, serving 11 years total, two years as the council president. During that time, he ran for—but lost—the race for the 7th Congressional District to fellow Democrat Jim McDermott.

Rice won plaudits for his successes on the city council. He had successfully supervised the city's budget, developed rate design for Seattle City Light, and gained passage of the Women and Minority

Business Enterprise (WMBE) ordinance, as well as working to disinvest city funds from South Africa during apartheid.

Accomplishments aside, Rice's second try at running for mayor was no shoo-in. The field of a dozen contenders included formidable opponents. Among them were former Seattle Councilmember Randy Revelle and City Attorney Doug Jewett, a so-called moderate Republican and a prime backer of Initiative 34, the Save Our Schools measure.

In the September primary, Rice and Jewett emerged as finalists, with Jewett slightly ahead. But, while the school busing controversy launched the mayoral race, crime became the bigger campaign issue. There was a feeling in city neighborhoods that people were threatened; they wanted more security. Rice campaigned promising that, if elected, he'd raise the city's business and occupation taxes and hire 102 more police officers.

Seattle voters turned the contest into a runaway election for Norm, and the national press took notice. It was newsworthy that, in a city with only a 10 percent black population, he had become the city's first black mayor by a wide margin, 58 to 42 percent. He had soundly defeated an avid anti-busing advocate. (At the same time the anti-busing measure passed narrowly, only to be set aside later by the school district commissioners.) Speaking of Norm's victory, his campaign manager Charles Rolland wasn't shy. In his view: "Seattle set an example for the rest of the United States."

Little did the voters know that, in campaigning and winning decisively, Rice had relied on a secret background. His official biography detailed his upbringing in Colorado, youngest son of a Pullman porter and a beauty salon maid. His bio told how he entered but left the University of Colorado, unhappy with segregated housing and meal facilities. He arrived in Seattle in the late 1960s, first attending Highline Community College and enrolling at the University of Washington.

However, Rice's official biography neglected to make mention of some of his early training and ambitions. He was breaking ground as the city's first black mayor, but he also was the first former actor to hold the position.

Rice had been an aspiring actor in Denver. In his 20s, he was a student at a Colorado community college, doing odd jobs, reading electric meters, and working as a hospital orderly. Meanwhile, he was picking up acting assignments when and where he could.

Jonathan Parker, a colleague from those days, acted along with Rice in the 1960s. Parker later ran the Fine Arts Center at Denver University. There weren't many jobs for black actors at the time—except for those who could "pass" as whites.

Rice was "a good, maybe even a great actor," Parker told me. "He could handle difficult roles. He was an even keel fellow."

As the new mayor, Norm's skill at improvising in difficult situations would stand him in good stead. As a reporter covering civic events, I remember times when Rice would arrive late at an event with only minutes to spare. He would be handed a sketchy agenda, but would immediately address the audience, smoothly and professionally. It was the sort of thing that an experienced actor could handle.

When Rice stepped into the mayor's office following his election, there was an almost overnight change at City Hall. Ongoing tensions between the mayor and city council, rampant during other administrations, lessened noticeably. Some credit was due to the fact that Rice had been a councilmember for 11 years. He understood how to smooth over differences between the legislative and executive branches of government. He knew how government ought to work.

But credit for improved relations lay also with Rice's considerable ability as a consensus builder. A genial smile, the ability to listen, and the skill to work out compromises gave him the nickname of "Mayor Nice." When he left office, the *Seattle Times*, not always a Rice supporter, called him "one of the best mayors Seattle ever had." The paper noted he had the rare ability to win while not leaving opponents with a sense of loss.

That's not to say that Norm's two terms lacked challenges. Troubled public schools, human rights, drug abuse, crime, and homelessness were among the issues that Seattle, like many big cities, was facing.

One of Rice's early moves was to convene a city-wide Seattle Schools summit. Out of the summit came a plan for the Family and Education Levy, a $69 million, seven-year property tax levy approved in 1990 to augment school budgets and to raise money for nurses, counselors, and after-class supervision.

Equally important were Mayor Rice's concentrated efforts to save the city's retail core. The city center was in rapid decline. Frederick & Nelson, one of the city's largest department stores, was closing its doors. Other retail establishments were leaving or threatening to close. Downtown had become a civic disgrace with empty storefronts, boarded up buildings, and people sleeping in doorways.

Rice attacked the problem head on. He worked out a deal that had the city enter a private-public partnership with downtown developers. The plan was for the city to finance a six-level, 120-space parking garage. The underground garage was the key element in the Pacific Place development, leading to a redeveloped Nordstrom flagship store and a revitalized city center.

The deal was not without skeptics. Critics attacked Rice's use of federal Housing and Urban Development (HUD) funds earmarked for the nation's most blighted neighborhoods. Did downtown qualify as blighted? The media—led by the *Seattle Times*—closely followed the transaction, hinting that federal funds might have been misused.

Despite economic and fiscal challenges, Rice experienced no trouble winning reelection in 1993. Race had been a minor issue during his first mayoral campaign. By the time he ran for a second term, it appeared to be a non-issue. Rice's opponent, David Stern, an ad man who claimed credit for the "Smiley Face" icon, attacked Rice, branding him as soft on the issues of drug abuse, crime, and homelessness. Voters didn't buy Stern's charges. They overwhelmingly returned Mayor Nice to office for a second term.

Meanwhile, the city's approach to comprehensive land use planning was fast becoming a critical issue with neighborhood forces. Some communities were not pleased with becoming "urban villages," a designation that allows for higher density and more intense development.

Rice found himself taking heat from a variety of sources. Some disgruntled city employees were spreading unsubstantiated stories. There were rumors of corruption at City Hall, misdeeds at Seattle City Light, and a whispering campaign about predatory cops. One especially virulent rumor alleged a cover-up in the mayor's personal life.

A Seattle Water Department employee fired in 1993, Kurt Hettiger, undertook a campaign of accusation against Rice, distributing flyers throughout Seattle headlined, "Who Shot Mayor Norman B. Rice?" Substance of the false rumor was that Rice had been shot by his wife—or possibly another family member—when discovered in a sex act with his male deputy mayor.

The rumor was extensively investigated at both the *Times* and the *Post-Intelligencer*. Despite efforts of award-winning investigative reporters to discover even a single grain of evidence, the rumor was found completely without substance.

The *P-I*'s managing editor, Kenneth Bunting, said, "To believe the incident as Hettiger had detailed it, one had to also believe that the police department, emergency transport drivers, and the hospital had all engaged in an elaborate conspiracy to cover it up." The *Times*, too, discounted the phony rumor.

But rumors, even without a shred of evidence, die hard. On a spring day in 1995, shortly after Rice announced his campaign for governor, a caller revived the rumor on Mike Siegel's "Hot Talk" show on KVI-AM. Siegel let the caller, a dismissed Seattle police officer, ramble on without interruption. Siegel promised to look into the rumor. He hired his own private investigator who, once again, found the rumor without substance.

Over the next several weeks, conservative talk shows throughout the state focused on the newly revived rumor. How to scotch the false rumor? Finally the mayor decided to respond publicly. While serving as president of the U.S. Conference of Mayors in May 1995, Rice held a press conference. The hope was that, aired and denied, the unverified rumor would die a natural death.

At the extraordinary press conference, Mayor Rice called the rumor "ludicrous, outrageous and untrue." He said his first response was to ignore the rumor. But he had decided to issue a denial because of the hurt done to his wife and son. His wife, Dr. Constance Rice, made a surprise appearance at the press conference. In an emotional statement, she said that she could never have been involved in a shooting. She said she hated guns and revealed the reason for her strong aversion: Her own father had been murdered by a gunman.

In the aftermath, the *Seattle P-I* ran a 35-inch, front-page story that referenced the substance of the rumor while, at the same time, thoroughly discounting it. The *Times* ran its story inside, referring vaguely to "bizarre rumors about the mayor's personal life."

Figuring he had done his best to stem rumors, Rice took off on a statewide tour, campaigning hard for governor. He dubbed the tour "Taking the High Road with Rice." But despite his best efforts, Rice lost the September 1996 Democratic primary to King County Executive Gary Locke. At the same time, Rice tallied more votes than the top GOP candidate. Some years later, the question of the rumor's lingering effect led to a national discussion of how the media should handle such stories. The Poynter Institute, known as a watchdog for the journalism profession, ran a case study devoted specifically to the Mayor Rice rumor.

Joann Byrd, former *Everett Herald* editor and a visiting ethics professional at Poynter, framed the discussion: "When someone is spreading a false rumor in order to get attention, it creates a dilemma—should you confront the rumor head-on, even if it gives the perpetrator the attention he wants? Or should you ignore the rumor, even if it means that some people may wonder if it's true?"

At the Poynter Institute, media experts came down on both sides. They issued a report headlined, "We Don't Do Rumors: But Sometimes, It Might Not Hurt." The Poynter assessment was clear that the media should not report rumors that cannot be verified. But the report cited unusual cases such as this one—with Mayor Rice himself referencing the rumor. In such instances, media could perform a public service by branding the rumor false and unsubstantiated. Discrediting a rumor, said the experts, might actually kill it.

Yet it was understandable that, after two successful but stressful terms, Rice might not relish a third term. Widely thought to be the likely candidate to head the U.S. Department of Housing and Urban Development under President Bill Clinton, Rice instead accepted the job of CEO and then president of the Federal Home Loan Bank of Seattle.

After six years at the Home Loan Bank, he left in 2004 to accept a post at the University of Washington Evans School of Public Affairs.

In 2009, he was named CEO of the Seattle Foundation, one of the city's oldest and largest charities. He is credited with helping the foundation target important social and human services and with enlisting a growing number of young philanthropists. He also gets credit for initiating the "Giving Big" campaign that brought $25 million to local charities.

Praising Norm's career when he decided to leave the Seattle Foundation, the *Times* declared: "Taking a city where it is destined to go is part leadership and part consensus building. Rice was good at it; he saved downtown." The *Times* also editorialized that, "if any city or organization needs a visionary, coaxing Rice out of retirement would be a tempting idea."

8

Writes of Passage, 1991

I wrote my last column for the *Post-Intelligencer* just prior to April Fool's Day 1991. Some may regard that day as significant.

Leaving the paper was a surprise to many, most of all to me. I had always thought that I would work at the *P-I* as long as they would have me. But I had been offered an opportunity to take my four-day-a-week city column, a mix of news, personalities, and Seattle stories, to the rival *Times*.

Part of the reason for parting company with the *P-I* after 17 eventful years was that I was marketable. As a city columnist, I had been appearing regularly in an anchor spot—right-hand column on B1, the local page—along with a half-column mug shot. I had high readership numbers after eight years as a columnist, right up there with local sports columns. Given that profile, I was able to make the switch, unlike many of my far more talented but less known colleagues.

Newspaper economics were trending downward in 1991. In years past, newspaper profits—increasing 5 percent or more per year— seemed solid. Now profits were beginning to shrink. Newspapers were cutting back, laying off staff, and reducing news-gathering budgets. The rise of television news was affecting the bottom line. Equally ominous were sharp declines in advertising revenues.

What was happening nationally was also evident in Seattle. Population in the region was growing, but newspaper circulation had remained static. Subscribers were aging and younger readers were hard to corral. Papers kept adding youth bait—reviews of rock concerts and lifestyle trends—to no avail. Youth readership lagged dismally.

We first noticed the coming crisis in February 1991 when we heard about the drastic double-digit cuts that the Hearst Corporation, the *P-I*'s parent company, was demanding of the *San Francisco Examiner*, the chain's flagship newspaper. Austerity was in the air and the *P-I* and other Hearst publications would undoubtedly be next to feel the budget axe.

P-I Publisher Virgil Fassio made the layoff announcement early in March, standing at the City Desk beside Executive Editor J. D. Alexander. Fassio said that there would be buy-outs and bonuses. He said that, if enough employees agreed to buy-outs, there would be no need for layoffs. Otherwise there would be reductions in force. Under the union contract, the last hired employees would be first to go.

Pressed for details, the publisher said there would be a 10 percent reduction in the news force. That meant as many as 12 staffers would be gone. The *P-I*, as always, had a significantly smaller staff than the rival *Times*. How could the leaner, feistier paper compete equipped with an even more depleted staff?

Fassio, the grim messenger, faced the news room and did not mince words. "Some of you have been here for years," he said. "You've had your chance. You have a duty to take the payoff, move on and make room for new, younger staffers."

It was a very sad day at the paper. It was particularly poignant since some of the paper's newcomers had only recently been hired from other newsrooms. The new arrivals were young journalists beginning their careers. They had quit secure positions to come to Seattle. They had been forced to deal with what, even at that time, seemed like high housing costs. Many had uprooted their families to make the move. Finally settled in Seattle and now, as the latest arrivals, they were targeted for job loss.

Over the next couple of days, I came to dread a trip to the women's restroom. I was sure to run into a new colleague sobbing over the prospect of losing her job.

"I'm number 9," said one young woman. "What are the odds? Not a chance in the world that my job can be saved." Gloom surrounded us like an impenetrable November fog.

As a long-time employee, I was not immediately impacted. But I was conflicted. I had been approached more than once by *Times* staff wondering about my loyalty to the *P-I*. There was a recent chamber of commerce event where I encountered *Times* President Mason Sizemore. He had asked, "Isn't it time you took your column to a real paper?"

Was it an actual job offer or a joking dig, the kind of crack newsies often directed at one another? I hadn't tried to find out. One reason for my failure to investigate prospects was that the *P-I* was a morning paper, whereas the *Times* was still an afternoon paper. I was convinced that the kind of chatty city column that I wrote worked best in the morning over coffee, rather than appearing at day's end.

I had the sinking feeling that it must be too late. I ought to have explored the opportunity to switch papers earlier. With newspapers cutting back nationally, the *Times* would also be trimming. The paper we called "Fairview Fanny" was not going to do much hiring in 1991. Many of my colleagues, the best and the brightest, had already fled to the larger newspaper. Over the past years, the shift had been notable. Among those who had jumped ship were Duff Wilson, Casey Corr, Mary Rothschild, and Eric Nalder.

Emmett Watson, the city's premier columnist, had earlier parted company with the *P-I*. After completing a memoir (*Digressions of a Native Son*) Watson had rejoined the *Times'* staff. (A chain-smoker, he said of his return to his former digs: "I just went out for a pack of cigarettes.")

The usual route between the two papers had been for journalists to start at the *Post-Intelligencer*, the younger, bolder paper. Once established, they would allow themselves to be lured away by the *Times*, a newspaper with a larger local circulation.

It was a gloomy March morning—one of a chain of them—and I was at my desk writing, still kicking myself for missing the chance to explore a move to the *Times*. Out of the blue my phone rang. It was a call from Mindy Cameron, the *Times'* editorial page editor.

"Wondered if you'd like to have lunch with Mike Fancher," said Cameron, referring to the *Times'* executive editor. I gulped so hard that I was sure that she could hear my discomfort over the phone.

"Uh yes," I said, my voice reduced to a croak. A thousand thoughts raced through my head. I was finally able to ask, "When would Fancher like to meet?"

"Later this week," said Cameron. "How about Thursday?" The oddity of the *Times* editorial page editor arranging a lunch between an executive editor and a rival columnist gave rise to another flash of thoughts. I suddenly realized that I was sitting at the very same desk, the desirable one in the corner of the newsroom, where first Casey Corr and then Mary Rothschild had worked before leaving the *P-I*.

"Can we make it Thursday noon at Kamon on Lake Union?" I suggested, mentioning a sushi restaurant close to the *Times*.

"Done," said Cameron. I felt as if the word applied to my goose cooking. But it was too late to back out now that I had agreed to meet with the top gun in the *Times* newsroom. I was reminded that a former co-worker once said that "if you talk, you'll walk."

When I arrived at Kamon, I found not one but two men waiting for me: Mike Fancher and Alex MacLeod, the *Times* managing editor. We exchanged pleasantries—weather (soggy) and politics (teacher salary raises)—and then ordered sushi from the appealing Japanese menu.

While still waiting for our meal, Fancher got right to the point, asking, "What would it take to persuade you to move your column to the *Seattle Times*?"

In the last day or two I had given the matter some thought, but I hadn't expected to have to come up with a proposal before our food was even delivered. I hadn't said a word to my closest friends at the *P-I*, although I did mention my lunch date to Alex Edelstein who had become a special friend following the death of my husband. Alex had been chair of the University of Washington Department of Communication and had once been a newsman himself.

In any event, I believed I should keep any terms simple and modest. I decided to pick only three considerations.

"I would like to keep my seniority," I said. "I've worked my way up to a four-week vacation each year and would hate to go back to a two-week minimum."

I next asked for a seat in the newsroom, something that seemed essential for a columnist writing about city events. To me, being shut away in an office would hardly work. At the *P-I*, I had been physically part of the newsroom, picking up column tips from seatmates, gossip from colleagues and sometimes pitching in along with reporters to cover breaking events.

"Finally," I said, still trying to gauge my lunch companions' reaction, "I need to be paid the same as the male columnists. That's not the case at the *P-I*. When I went through newspaper guild records, I discovered my pay was lower than the paper's five male columnists."

After our meals were served, Fancher said, "I believe we can meet those terms. The only tough part will be finding a seat in the crowded newsroom."

Afterwards, I sat for a time in my car, aghast at what I had just done. I realized that I had made my bed, as they say. I had agreed to write a column for the *Times*. I felt a little queasy, but I found a measure of comfort knowing that, at the very least, I would be saving one *P-I* job from the publisher's 10 percent reduction in force.

The only thing left to discuss now was the timing. I figured I would be submitting a letter of resignation to the *P-I*, cleaning out my desk and then taking a couple of unpaid weeks off, maybe a quick vacation, before starting at the *Times*.

The really tough part would be telling my friends and co-workers. Colleagues become close in a newsroom. It's like a long and mostly good marriage: Putting out a daily paper together, working alongside one another, discovering one another's idiosyncrasies, surviving petty quarrels, and overhearing family communications. Leaving the newspaper would be like a divorce and not a particularly friendly one, since I was leaving to work for a rival publication.

Sure I'd still see my closest *P-I* friends, buddies like Mary Lynn Lyke, Carol Smith, Nancy Hevly, Bruce Ramsey, Jane Hadley, Don Carter, Grant Haller, Lytt Smith, Shelby Scates, David Horsey, Janet Grimley, and Susan Phinney. The list was long, almost the entire masthead. I loved them all. We might still get together, but the bond wouldn't be the same.

My coworkers at the *P-I* and I had laughed together, broken bread over lunches, cried over lost colleagues, and gasped at breaking news events. Together we had experienced the resignation of Richard Nixon, the selection of vice presidential candidate Geraldine Ferraro, the rise of AIDS, the freeing of Poland under Solidarity, and the *Exxon Valdez* running aground in Prince William Sound in Alaska. During the *P-I* years I had graduated my sons, lost my husband to multiple sclerosis, sold my home, and bought another. My co-workers had shared my life just as I had shared theirs.

First order of business the next morning was to take my formal letter of resignation to J. D. Alexander, the executive editor. When others had made the move between papers, there had often been a period of negotiation—perhaps the offer of a bigger salary or a more challenging beat. In my case, that was not to be.

Alexander, a *Washington Post* line editor during Watergate, was a large man—not tall, but broad, built like an apprentice lineman. He used his bulk to intimidate. I had always believed that he had only just tolerated me, although he had moved my column from the features section to a prime spot on the local news pages.

When I submitted my letter of resignation, he didn't seem surprised or displeased. Nor did he try to dissuade me from leaving, although he confirmed that I wouldn't qualify for a buyout. It was almost as if he already had a possible replacement in mind. He merely wished me well and said that, no, I didn't have to wait the customary two weeks after giving notice, I should leave immediately.

My goodbye to Fassio didn't go as smoothly. The publisher appeared aggrieved when I said that I was going to the *Times*. He said, "I have worked at other papers, but I have never, ever walked across the street." At a loss for words, I did manage to point out, somewhat weakly, that he had told the long-time employees to "move on." He concluded with angry words: "We gave you your chance." There wasn't much left but to say goodbye and tell him that it had been "a great privilege to work at the *P-I*."

I gathered my personal belonging from my desk. I had taken my Rolodex home the previous day, not sure whether or not someone would claim it as *P-I* property. My contacts were my most valuable asset and I would have hated to reconstruct that phone list from scratch.

Several colleagues insisted that I meet them after work for a final toast before leaving the paper and I foolishly agreed. I had arranged to meet a *Times* photographer for a picture session, leaving me an hour before my 7 p.m. appointment. Unhappily I relaxed and allowed a single glass of wine to become two. I forgot that I didn't have a head for alcohol and that I needed to exercise restraint.

When I reached the *Times*, the photographer snapped the mug shot to accompany a front-page announcement that I would be writing for the paper. The headline read: "Jean Godden Moves to the *Times.*" My focus was a little bleary, my smile a little broad. That would be my column shot for the next year, something to remind me of my alcoholic folly.

The *Times* editors, including my new boss City Editor Dave Boardman, had been adamant that I skip a vacation and take only three days off before writing my first column. It was more difficult than I thought. After appearing in *Times* headlines as something of a trophy, what does one say? I finally decided to be completely honest, come clean about the business of authoring a column. I wrote:

> Columnists are the oddballs of the newspaper. They're neither the hard-hitting reporters who daily play stop-the-presses nor the deep-thinking editorialists who prefer to say such things as "on the one hand" and "on balance." A friend once told me that his editor described a columnist as "just another clerk who got lucky."
>
> Turns out the "lucky clerk" thing is the business I have been in for the past eight years, writing for Brand Y.
>
> The other day I struck it luckier. I was asked to write a column for the *Seattle Times.* It was a proud moment and a scary one, because— just between us—there's always the worry that you could misplace the knack. It's like wondering if you would remember the recipe for ice cubes if you suddenly moved to Olympia and were having the governor in for ice tea.
>
> So much for self-doubt. I have the notion that I should explain what this column will be like. That's so you can skip it if you're looking for fashion tips, meeting notices or advice on how to paper-train the dog.
>
> The column mainly will report items about people around Puget Sound, about politicians, plumbers, poets and panhandlers. It probably won't say anything unkind about cats. I know enough to keep out of real trouble.
>
> It's inevitable that the column will occasionally report real news. Left alone with voice mail and a word processor, anything is possible.
>
> I like to "talk Seattle," explain to newcomers what the natives mean when they say "Boeing time" (a work day that starts at 6 a.m.) or "perfect day" (70 degrees and partly sunny with a fresh breeze from the north).
>
> If I have a prejudice, and who doesn't, it's that I don't admire people who flock to Puget Sound because they like the lifestyle and then try to change the city's character. This area is special. The worst thing that could happen to Seattle would be to become bland, another Anywhere U.S.A.

Those paragraphs are taken from my first *Seattle Times* column. It appeared Sunday, April 7, breaking the ice and any excuse for writers' block.

I arrived at the paper on Monday morning, April 8. I was given a photo I.D. card and introduced to the important people: my new editor, Bill Ristow, City Editor Dave Boardman, and most notable of all, Marge Ceccarelli, the office manager who ran things her way. We called her "Marge the Sarge."

Best of all, I was assigned a seat in the newsroom. Mine was located in a far corner of the room, right next to the copy aides' station, back to back with science reporter Diedtra Henderson. The copy aides were constantly in and out, making deliveries, doing pick-ups. I was seated in the ideal place for getting the freshest news of the day.

9

The Battle of Seattle, 1999

It was the evening of November 30, 1999, when Keiko Morris burst into the *Seattle Times* city room half blinded by streams of stinging tears. The youthful reporter had been out on the streets most of the day covering anti-World Trade Organization riots. She told those of us working at our newsroom desks that she had been hit with a faceful of tear gas.

I followed Keiko into the restroom to help bathe her eyes. Washing with tap water seemed to help. But then she lamented, "My hair. Look at my hair. It's full of tear gas; feel it."

Keiko's short Afro had absorbed the chemical spray, soaking it up like a sponge. I took a tentative feel and then recoiled, my hand dripping with the toxic liquid. I had inadvertently sprayed second-hand tear gas all over the women's restroom. My eyes began burning and my cheeks, too, were flooded with tears.

We would smell and fight that sharp, noxious odor on the streets of Seattle and in our poorly insulated offices throughout the week while WTO battles waged around us. It was a war the world would follow on live television, tarring a city that had naïvely longed to appear "world class."

The main goal of the WTO's third ministerial conference, scheduled in Seattle the last year of the twentieth century, was to work out a global agenda for trade negotiations. The agreement would extend into the new millennium. But before the ministers could hold opening ceremonies at the Paramount Theatre on the morning of November 30, protests already were raging in the streets.

Tens of thousands—estimates ranged from 50,000 to 100,000—converged on downtown Seattle. The protesters represented broadly different interests, some labor, some environmental, some philosophical. But there was a common anti-globalization thrust. Instead of World Trade Organization, some mockingly called it "World Take-

Over." Opposition led to raucous battles between hordes of protesters and a seemingly over-militarized Seattle police force.

As a *Times* columnist, I first learned about the WTO conference the previous summer. During a Seattle Port Commission meeting, Commissioner Pat Davis casually described the conference as "an exciting event that will be happening later this year." Davis said there would be delegates from 134 countries, as well as dozens of heads of state and hundreds of observers. They were scheduled to visit the city in late November and early December.

Davis foresaw the hundreds of multinational delegates doing their Christmas shopping in Seattle stores. She noted that trade agreements hammered out in Seattle would become known as "the Seattle Round." She thought the conference would establish the city's reputation as a trade-oriented center.

All this enthusiasm totally neglected mention of what had happened at a previous meeting of WTO ministers. During the Geneva meeting in May 1998, a crowd of 4,000 showed up to protest, burning cars and smashing windows.

Nevertheless, during that same conference, President Bill Clinton warmly invited the WTO to hold its next meeting in the United States. He issued the invitation but left details and arrangements to the State Department.

Seattle was one of 21 U.S. cities that quickly expressed interest in hosting. After a lengthy screening process, the State Department narrowed the field to Seattle and Honolulu and asked for more detailed proposals. The city's case was pushed by a Seattle host committee that included Seattle Mayor Paul Schell, Washington Governor Gary Locke, King County Executive Ron Sims, Boeing's Phil Condit, and Microsoft's Bill Gates. The state's congressional delegation lobbied on the city's behalf. With such high-powered help, Seattle came out on top.

Based on an earlier experience with the APEC (Asian Pacific Economic Conference), a meeting held on nearby Blake Island in 1993, officials here estimated security might cost as much as $500,000. Planners later upped that estimate, figuring that security could run as high as $1.5 million. Yet the projected cost did not trouble the host committee nor Davis's trade group. They expected costs would mainly be borne by the U.S. government. Besides, Davis reported, local corporations would raise cash for the conference, perhaps as much as $9 million.

By the time the Seattle City Council was consulted, somewhat belatedly, councilmembers asked pointed questions about police expenses. Their qualms were dismissed by the mayor's office. Despite assurances, the council asked for a memorandum of understanding (MOU) over who would pay how much and for what. Councilmembers later learned to their dismay that the MOU request was never taken seriously by the city's Office of Intergovernmental Relations. According to Director Cliff Traisman, it was the sort of agreement that should have been negotiated prior to the city's selection.

So much for financial concerns. Planning for security deployment was another critical matter. At the time, Seattle had only 1,060 police officers, a force that had to be divided into three eight-hour shifts. Given required days off, the department normally could field only 400 police per shift as a maximum. It was a very thin blue line.

Police Chief Norm Stamper sidestepped direct involvement, leaving security planning to Deputy Chief Ed Joiner. Neither Stamper nor Joiner pressed for a higher overtime budget. There were attempts to train the Seattle police force, but, given the size of the conference and the magnitude of the task, preparations fell far short.

Chief Stamper showed up to review instructions provided to Seattle Police Department (SPD) officers. Police training, such as it was, culminated in a mock protest demonstration (police versus police) held in an abandoned hangar at Sand Point, a former U.S. Naval Air Station on Lake Washington. By staggering and adjusting shifts, 900 uniformed cops would be placed on WTO duty, more than had been fielded at any one time in the department's history. Chief Stamper concluded, "We've got this sucker covered."

Mayor Schell too seemed unconcerned. In his own words, he described what he expected: "The police will make sure that, for citizens of this city, life can go on more or less as usual. The carousel will be up at Westlake; shoppers will fill the stores; the holiday lights will be up, and the ballet will be dancing 'The Nutcracker.' This is still Seattle in December after all."

City leaders assumed it would be business as usual. They neglected and all but dismissed security risks. Meanwhile, opposition forces were far more engaged. Protesters were mobilizing via the internet, making plans to disrupt the conference. For many, the avowed goal was nothing less than shutting down the WTO conference.

The Ruckus Society, a nonprofit group dedicated to workers' rights and environmental justice, had set up an action camp. Trainers were schooling protesters in non-violent disruptive techniques: how to block streets and sidewalks and how to hang opposition banners.

Also preparing to shut down the conference were Black Bloc anarchists. The militant, anti-government bloc members had plans to travel north from their base in Eugene, Oregon, dressed in all-black clothing and masks. Trained in property destruction, their targets included federal buildings and national chains.

Despite repeated warnings from Oregon authorities that trouble was inevitable, Seattle had made no solid plans to combat massive civil disobedience. In fact, the city had already dismissed early offers of mutual assistance from neighboring police forces. When King County proposed loaning 114 deputies, Seattle leaders, concerned with escalating costs, turned the offer down.

Protests started early. On the morning of Friday, November 26, three days before the conference was due to start, an estimated 50 protesters marched through downtown, disrupting traffic and breaking windows. By afternoon a larger crowd gathered at Westlake Center with some members splitting off, trying to enter the Convention Center.

Saturday, too, brought pre-WTO opposition with three people arrested for rappelling down a wall and hanging an anti-WTO banner "No to WTO" on Interstate-5. A few dozen people established a demonstration headquarters at Fourth and East Denny.

The protesters were a multi-faceted group, made up mainly of labor and environmental organizations opposed to unfettered free trade. The Direct Action Network, an umbrella organization, enlisted many WTO opponents, including student groups and religious organizations. Prepared in advance were banners that proclaimed: "Global Injustice," "No WTO," and "Make Trade Clean, Green." Labor forces believed globalization would lead to lower U.S. wages and lost jobs. Environmental opponents feared "a race to the bottom," eroding environmental standards.

Police officers met Sunday to discuss a request from the Ruckus Society that a thousand demonstrators be arrested on Tuesday. Mass arrests were one tactic used by the society to publicize its opposition message. However, during the meeting it soon became plain to all that the police did not have the manpower or jail capacity to handle a thousand protesters. The Ruckus representatives left saying they'd have to "do something else" to get their message out.

That afternoon, a group of some 500 started a march along Broadway. Escorted by police, they marched downtown with the intent of shutting down The Gap clothing store. After blocking downtown streets, the protesters demanded and got an escort back to Seattle Community College. Worrisome reports surfaced, including word from the Broadway Fred Meyer that protesters had purchased all that store's lighter fluid.

By Sunday evening, Seattle police learned from media that protesters had taken over the Kalberer Building at Ninth and Virginia Street to use as a command center. Reports said they were nailing building doors shut from the inside.

Protest activity started early on Monday, November 29. At 4 a.m., five members of the Rainforest Action Network climbed a towering construction crane near I-5. They unfurled a giant anti-WTO banner that showed two opposing arrows, one labeled "Democracy." The other arrow, pointed in the opposite direction, was labeled "WTO."

That morning the Sierra Club held a peaceful march. By afternoon hundreds had gathered at the First Methodist Church at Fifth and Marion. Swelling to over a thousand, the crowd began wandering through downtown and ignoring police orders to disperse. One group converged on the McDonald's at Third and Pine, smashing windows and spray-painting walls. A police car was also sprayed.

In the evening, a group of religious leaders held an anti-WTO prayer meeting, drawing an estimated 5,000 people. This group then marched to the Stadium Exhibition Center just north of Safeco Field, where WTO ministers were attending a pre-conference reception.

The demonstrators, joined by labor forces, forged a human chain around the center, hurling rocks and targeting police with laser pointers. AFL-CIO organizers repeatedly called for non-violence, but they were shouted down.

Across town several thousand activists showed up for a "People's Gala" at KeyArena on the Seattle Center grounds. Mayor Schell attended, urging the crowd to "be tough on your issues, but be gentle on my town."

Protesters began assembling in locations near the Convention Center as early as 2 a.m. on opening day of the conference, Tuesday, November 30—a date Seattleites would refer to as "N-30." By 7:30 a.m., the center was completely surrounded by thousands converging from four different directions. Protesters chained themselves to manholes, set fire to debris at Eighth and Seneca, and pushed a dumpster into the street on Olive Way. One hundred demonstrators lay down at Sixth and Pine while others attacked cars, damaged property, and stretched chains across the intersection at Ninth and Olive.

Members of the SPD's First Watch Task Force, the early morning shift, were diverted and reassigned to crowd management. That shift went without relief, without rest or meal breaks, and had to contend with large-scale disturbances. Hundreds marched from the Pike Place Public Market to Sixth and Olive Way where they chained themselves together. Other protesters, the notorious Black Bloc, began smashing windows at Niketown, Nordstrom, and Planet Hollywood, using crowbars and masonry hammers.

By 8:30 a.m. an estimated 30 activists, some wearing gas masks, locked themselves inside plastic sewer pipes at Sixth and Pike, opposite the Sheraton Hotel where many of the dignitaries were staying. A crowd gathered and started hurling debris. At the same time, around 20 black-clad rioters were seen throwing newspaper boxes into the intersection. When the rioters were chased away, they fled toward the Washington Athletic Club and were joined by 50 or more anarchists.

Concerned by delegates' reports of harassment, Seattle police made the decision to lock down both the Sheraton and the Convention Center. Officers discovered evidence of a break-in at the Center that necessitated another search of the facility. There was concern that

WTO protestors, attired as sea turtles, represent the Animal Welfare Institute, November 29, 1999. *Seattle Municipal Archives, Item 175624*

militants would set off fire sprinklers, flood the interior, and set off stink bombs or, worse, real bombs.

The WTO's opening ceremonies were an early casualty. First the ceremonies were postponed; later they were abruptly cancelled.

Incredibly in the midst of all this disorder, the Sierra Club managed to hold a peaceful march from Denny Park to the Seattle Center. A march from Seattle Community College to the Center also got underway, as did a previously scheduled AFL-CIO march.

Some 250 of the marchers wore sea turtle outfits, designed and constructed by environmental activist Ben White of the Sea Shepherd Society. White took his idea from the World Trade Organization's axing of a U.S. law that required shrimpers to construct their nets so that sea turtles could not be entangled. White thought people would identify with the urge to save the endangered species.

At one point during the sea turtle march, White jumped up onto a flatbed truck and shouted to all who could hear: "Welcome to the Revolution!"

At a few minutes after 9 a.m. on N-30, the SPD field commander authorized the use of chemical agents and the department made a frantic call for mutual aid. The police were still trying to clear a path along Union and University to the Convention Center, giving the crowd repeated warnings to disperse. Warnings went unheeded.

Police had to rescue 20 WTO delegates at Sixth and Union after they were surrounded and held hostage by protesters. The incident prompted the Seattle host organization to advise delegates to remain in their hotels until order could to be restored. Among those trapped: Secretary of State Madeleine Albright.

First use of chemical weapons was not by police, but by a protester who sprayed 13 officers with pepper spray at 9:30 a.m. Soon after, police began using chemical agents on protesters who were refusing to clear Union and University. Even with the use of tear gas and pepper spray, police realized they could not hold both streets and had to abandon University in an effort to hold Union.

While looters rampaged throughout downtown vandalizing patrol cars and throwing barricades through windows, SPD brass met with Mayor Schell to request a civil emergency declaration, a curfew order, and help from the National Guard.

The mayor finally obliged. He declared the civil emergency at 4:30 that afternoon. The order established a 7:00 p.m. to 7:30 a.m. curfew in the area bounded by Denny, Yesler, I-5, and Elliott Bay. Governor Locke simultaneously authorized deployment by the National Guard.

In the early evening of November 30, crowds on Pine and Pike Streets between Fourth and Sixth Avenues turned violent. They began throwing debris, breaking windows, and setting fires. Police responded, lining Cherry Street from First to Fifth, and driving protesters up Capitol Hill.

Police shadowed the crowd during the march up the hill, which led to an ugly standoff. Officers came under attack by an array of missiles, including golf balls, concrete chunks, bottles, traffic cones, ball bearings, and human urine shot from high powered squirt guns. Protesters set fire to trash bins near the Egyptian Theatre on East Pine Street, blocking the street with dumpsters. Gas-masked protesters fired their own tear gas at police officers who responded in kind. Diners in Capitol Hill cafés were gassed along with the rioters.

Mayor Schell and Chief Stamper held a news conference, admitting that they had been caught off guard by the sheer number of protesters. Stamper said he was afraid that his cops were "out there taking a licking." He said nonviolent protesters, store owners, workers, and shoppers were facing danger and that President Bill Clinton, who was headed to Seattle, might not be able to address the conference or even manage to reach the city center.

On the morning of Wednesday, December 1, *Times* editorialist Casey Corr and I left our offices and with press credentials walked past police lines to check out damage. We reached Sixth and Union, ground zero in the battle. Shops decorated for Christmas and trees festooned with Christmas lights were a stark contrast to the standoff on the ground—cops on one side and protesters on the other.

We found the air heavy with the acrid odors and choking clouds of chemical spray. Billows of smoke drifted from fires set by demonstrators at Westlake Center. There was an ominous feel to the atmosphere.

"This is like nothing I've ever seen or thought I would ever see," said one bystander, a displaced shopkeeper. Office workers caught up in the melee clustered together on the sidewalk.

From the Sixth Avenue sidewalk, we could see a narrow line of uniformed police stretched across the east (Union Street) side of the intersection. The police, outfitted with new equipment, displayed all-black hard gear with catcher-like shin guards and ballistic helmets, batons at their sides. To me they looked like extras from a Star Wars movie.

Casey Corr pointed out Captain Jim Pugel, the incident commander, who was standing in the forefront of the police line, a force of perhaps 100 that included mounted officers from the city's horse patrol.

Across the street were protesters, a motley throng that included young men wearing protective bandanas and Palestinian scarves, black-clad anarchists, the occasional marcher still wearing a battered sea turtle costume, brawny dock workers, and young women in ski jackets and jeans.

Mounted police and WTO protestors, November 29, 1999. *Seattle Municipal Archives, Item 176741*

The Sixth and Union intersection was suddenly filled by a surge of about 100 activists erupting from the crowd. Twenty protesters, using the mob as a screen, plopped down in the center of the road and hooked their arms together with chains threaded through concrete pipes.

Pugel raised a bullhorn to announce that the intersection must be cleared immediately.

He warned, "Those who fail to leave will be arrested." Police moved forward to take into custody those who remained seated. Given the rigid pipes and the risk of breaking protesters' arms, the task was daunting and time-consuming.

About 200 demonstrators, some with minor injuries, were finally led away. They were taken to nearby police buses, bound for Sand Point where they were processed in the former naval air station brig before being taken to the King County Jail. Given the limited manpower assigned to the task, processing was slow. Those arrested would spend hours huddled aboard police buses. The brig had only two phones, poorly functioning toilets, and undrinkable water.

Mayor Schell issued a second civil emergency order, banning protests around the Convention Center area, a zone bordered by Boren, Seneca, Fourth Avenue, and Lenora, now patrolled by armored trucks.

In U.S. District Court, the ACLU petitioned for a temporary injunction against the civil emergency order. A police commander had to leave patrol duties to provide a response summarizing the department's need for such an order. The court denied the ACLU petition.

During the night Air Force One with President Bill Clinton aboard touched down at Boeing Field. Thanks to the curfew order, the president and his party were able to reach the Westin Hotel without incident. Clinton spoke at the next day's WTO luncheon calling for moderation.

"We must deal with the legitimate concerns of the protesters, but we need to make an honest distinction between what we condemn and that which we welcome," said the president. His words had the ring of accommodation, offered too little, too late.

Protests continued throughout the afternoon with splinter groups blocking streets, trapping citizens in their cars, and damaging property. When another group occupied the Third and Pike intersection, the police once again resorted to use of chemical agents. More arrests followed.

At around 7 p.m., driving to a WTO event, Councilmember Richard McIver was stopped by police who refused to believe that he, an African American, was a city official. Stopped for a second time, McIver handed the officer his city business card. Despite his protests, he was commanded to stand against his car, hands behind his back. He was searched and his cell phone removed. He saw his business card thrown thoughtlessly to the ground. McIver never forgot the indignity. As long as he served in office, another 11 years, he was hostile to police budget requests.

Later that evening a police car trying to move through Broadway and Pine was attacked. Protesters swarmed over the vehicle, attempting to overturn it with officers inside. In response, the police fired concussion grenades and tear gas; protesters threw bottles, soup cans, bricks, and rocks from the ground and from nearby rooftops. The ensuing riot seesawed for five hours. Radio dispatchers received a report of a group taking over the Broadway Chevron station and filling bottles with gasoline.

A crowd of 1,500 descended on the East Precinct on Capitol Hill, surrounding the building and trying to break through the perimeter. In the early hours of the next morning, police used tear gas and rubber bullets to break up the mob of rioters. They finally scattered.

On December 2, a handful of downtown businesses opened in the restricted zone; some made plans to close early, while many remained shuttered. There were discussions of possible lawsuits to recover lost sales. The Downtown Seattle Association calculated that downtown businesses already had lost $7 million and likely would lose $2.5 million more per day.

That morning President Clinton left town and police evaluating the restricted zone eased the northern boundary without incident. Movement around the Convention Center began to improve too, although protests continued. One march from Seattle Central College to Victor Steinbrueck Park ended at the King County Jail. With the jail surrounded, officers placed the facility on lockdown. Police, consulting with Ruckus Society Director John Sellers, allowed two defense attorneys into the jail to check on conditions.

Later that day King County Executive Ron Sims and Sheriff Dave Reichert were traveling in a county car near the Pike Place Public Market. Reichert, who earlier had been highly critical of Mayor Schell's handling of the riots, spotted four looters fleeing from a RadioShack store. He called on the driver to pull the car over.

Sims later told reporters, "Dave said he couldn't take it any longer and out he went." Reichert leaped from the car and started running after the looters. Although Reichert failed to catch the criminals, he appeared on local television giving chase while tear gas fumes swirled around him. It was an immensely valuable photo opportunity for someone with political ambitions.

As downtown retailers started reopening on Friday, December 3, the city began to come under harsh criticism, much of it directed at Mayor Schell and his lack of preparedness. Sen. Slade Gorton praised the police, but heaped blame on city officials.

A noon march, organized by labor leaders, moved from the Labor Temple on Clay Street to Fifth and Pike. A crowd of around 500 broke off toward the Westin Hotel, perhaps thinking President Clinton was still there. They chained themselves to the Westin's doors. Later they joined a group protesting at the King County Jail.

During the clashes, media reported at least two incidents of police misconduct. At Pike Place Market an angry police officer kicked an unarmed demonstrator, striking him in the groin before shooting him in the chest with a rubber pellet.

Another confrontation took place on Capitol Hill when a police officer spotted a woman driver videotaping a protest action. He signaled her to roll down the car window. When she obeyed, the cop sprayed both the driver and her passenger with mace, shouting, "Now film this!"

Caught on TV cameras these two incidents would later be cited as evidence of a police force out of control. Investigators eventually would conclude—a small comfort—that neither of the rogue officers were Seattle police. Those officers were from suburban forces, pressed into service without time for proper training.

WTO organizers announced that evening that the trade ministers had been unable to overcome their differences; they would leave Seattle without starting a new round of trade agreements. Triumphant protest leader Mike Dolan of Ralph Nader's Public Citizen proclaimed, "The demonstrations were successful."

State Patrol and National Guard troops stood down on Saturday, December 4. Mayor Schell held a press conference at Westlake calling for "a time of healing." The ACLU and a coalition of local civil rights groups demanded an Independent Investigation of the handling of protest activities.

Also on Saturday, Police Chief Norm Stamper made the rounds of the still-operating command sites. Then he stopped at the Multi-Agency Command Center, where he told Deputy Mayor Maud Daudon that he was turning in his badge.

Stamper took responsibility for the debacle, saying he had been "snookered big time." In his book, *Breaking Rank*, written five years later, Stamper confessed, "To this day I feel pangs of regret."

In his book, Stamper lamented that his police officers had to spend long hours on the streets without adequate rest, sleep, bathroom breaks, or meals, absorbing threats and abuse. He expressed regret that local businesses were damaged and lost business during the rampage. Most of all, he was distressed that the city and the police department had forfeited their collective pride and lost self-confidence.

Finally, the former chief said he was sorry "that peaceful protesters failed to win an adequate hearing of their important anti-globalization message and that Paul Schell's dream of a citywide dialogue had been crushed."

In the aftermath of the WTO battle, the Seattle City Council appointed a special Accountability Review Committee. Co-chaired by Councilmembers Jim Compton, Jan Drago, and Nick Licata, the committee sought to assess what had occurred, what had gone wrong, and to make recommendations about future actions.

The committee's three panels, ably staffed by policy wonk Alec Fisken, faulted the city for failure to plan for such a large-scale demonstration, its tardiness in seeking mutual assistance, and the lack of council involvement in planning.

The committee cited disagreements between the city's police and fire departments that should have been addressed in advance. Among other requests, police had wanted firefighters' assistance in clearing intersections and uncoupling chained rioters. However, the fire department said its role should be confined to rescue, medical assistance, hazardous material identification, and fighting and preventing fires.

Post-WTO recommendations emphasized the need for a formal process, complete with citizen participation, and for the Seattle City Council's early involvement and full participation in any large-scale events, regardless of sponsorship. The committee recommended preparing for mass arrests. Better to arrest violent protesters, they believed, than to resort to widespread use of chemical weapons.

Despite good intentions and hopes behind the invitation to world trade ministers, the week of November 30 to December 3, 1999, and the ensuing WTO battle left scars on the city of Seattle.

Protesters were able to voice strong objection to the World Trade Organization, but much of the impact of their argument was dulled by press coverage of disruptions and damage. The image of Seattle as a progressive city, willing to accommodate divergent views, was badly tarnished and its leadership faulted.

For his role in the debacle, Mayor Paul Schell endured much criticism and condemnation, including cries for his resignation. Months later, while still seeking to explain his actions, Schell faced another disaster when an out-of-control Mardi Gras celebration in Pioneer Square resulted in the tragic death of a young man who tried to rescue a woman from attackers. Although the WTO riots had resulted in numerous injuries, there had been no fatalities.

The mayor had hoped to turn WTO into a responsible citizen dialogue ("be tough on your issues"), and he sought to show Seattle as a model of civility ("be kind to my city"). Instead, after his rocky four-year term, Schell lost his bid for reelection. He placed third on primary election day, September 18, 2001.

By contrast, Sheriff Dave Reichert parlayed the disaster to personal advantage. He had been highly critical of Mayor Schell's advance preparation for WTO, especially the mayor's early reluctance to seek additional help. The two officials exchanged harsh words. In the aftermath, Reichert faulted Mayor Schell's wait-and-see plan that, the sheriff claimed, "cost businesses more than $3 million."

In response, Schell called Reichert a "lunatic." The reference was to Reichert's personal pursuit of the Pike Place Market looters that, however ill-advised, had played so well on the 11 o'clock news. Reichert's proactive lawman stance helped him win a congressional seat, one that he held for 14 years. His name still is mentioned as a potential candidate for state elected offices.

Chief Stamper, years after quitting office, provided a view from his new perspective. By then, he had retired to a mountaintop on Orcas Island in the San Juan Islands. After he published his book the two of us had lunch at a restaurant near Seattle City Hall.

I took notes as he told me, "Seattle was too damned small to pull off an event like WTO. If you're thinking about such events you have to be able to count your cops in the thousands or tens of thousands, not hundreds. Hell, the city wouldn't have had enough cops if we'd called in every officer in the state."

The WTO conference and its aftermath remain a case study of overreach, mistakes, and lessons painfully learned. As a front-row witness to the Battle of Seattle, I had reported details such as Dave Reichert's pursuit of looters. I can relate to the sadness of Seattle leaders over the city's damaged image while at the same time, sympathize with peaceful demonstrators who marched as sea turtles and worked to preserve environmental standards and jobs. It was a tragedy that broader messages never emerged from the miasma of marches, riots, and overused chemical weapons.

10

49 Cold Days in Hell, 2000–2001

The night of Monday, November 20, 2000, was bitter cold and the mood combative as several hundred employees from the *Times* and *Post-Intelligencer* milled around outside the Bricklayers' Building on Fairview Avenue East. They were wrestling with a critical decision: To strike Seattle's two daily newspapers or not?

A loyal union member, I too was part of that crowd. Bundled to the teeth against the brisk wind gusts off Lake Union, I found myself next to David Postman, a colleague and top *Times* political reporter.

The December 15, 2000, issue of the *Guild Reporter* captured guild members picketing outside the *Seattle Times* offices. *Author's collection*

"They're not going to strike, are they?" Postman asked me. "You've got to stop them."

Postman argued in favor of the federal mediator's call for a 48-hour cooling off period rather than an immediate walkout. There was some sentiment, strongest among newsroom staffers, for a time out. The two newspapers had merged in a Joint Operating Agreement (JOA) in 1983. While there were totally separate newsrooms, the *Times* oversaw business operations for both papers.

Had I been inclined to advocate postponing a strike, it would have been little use. Newspaper employees, most of them underpaid circulation, advertising, and delivery workers, had many economic grievances. They were convinced management was not prepared to bargain and they had made up their minds. They—we—a thousand Pacific Northwest Newspaper Guild members (130 at the *P-I* and more than 900 at the *Times*) were going to walk out of the newsroom, out of classified and circulation offices, and off delivery trucks. And walk we did, most of us for seven long weeks, the coldest and cruelest winter I can remember in Seattle.

The 2000 newspaper strike was historic. It was the first since the Newspaper Guild struck the *Times* in 1953, the first Seattle newspaper strike in 47 years.

The 2000 strike had far-reaching consequences. It fractured the city's labor front. Some unions honored the strike; others crossed the picket lines. It led to Seattle briefly becoming a three-newspaper town. The *Union Record*, a strike paper published by union volunteers, was distributed three days a week, free throughout the city.

The strike was ruinous financially: workers who depended on a paycheck were forced to exist on strike pay, $200 a week for the first week; $300 a week thereafter. The papers were wounded by subscriber boycotts and ad cancellations during the holidays, their most lucrative season. The two companies were forced to distribute papers free and hire temporary workers to help short-handed management employees.

Strike preparations cost the papers dearly. At the *Times*, an expensive, ten-foot chain-link fence stretched around the block-square building. The newspaper hired an outside security force, looking, to us, like a cohort of ninja warriors. The guards patrolled the building and parking areas, and when things grew especially ugly, they chauffeured management employees to and from work. They were a constant presence on the rooftop, filming the picketing strikers.

Timing of the strike could scarcely have been worse. The struck newspapers were locked into a joint operating agreement that had left the *Times* responsible for all support functions. Despite the uneasy partnership, the two rivals were spoiling for a newspaper war, kicked off on May 6, 2000, when the *Times* switched from afternoon to morning delivery.

For those of us engaged in this head-to-head competition and now abruptly committed to a strike, it was a steep learning curve. We believed in collective bargaining; we knew we had the right to strike for better working conditions. What drove us to decide to walk was knowledge that wages were not keeping up with inflation, that health benefits were inadequate, and that suburban employees were being paid just 85 percent of downtown workers' wages.

While we knew we had reason to strike we knew next to nothing about how to go about managing a strike. We had gathered for a final debate at the King County Labor Temple, the building where many of us, as reporters, had covered other critical labor decisions.

The Labor Temple meeting drew naysayers, members who were opposed to a strike or at least against an immediate walk-out. The go-slow speeches came mainly from the downtown newsrooms, reporters who were treated marginally better than fellow unionists. The trouble was that, like most reporters, they loved their jobs so much that they would virtually have been willing to pay to do the work.

One highly ambivalent reporter, Lynda Mapes, took the mike and equivocated, saying, "I really think we need more time." She was interrupted by fist-pumping shouts of "No way!"

Moderation had no place the night of November 20. Dominated by circulation and advertising employees the room voted overwhelmingly in favor of an immediate walk-out. The vote was followed by a mass rally at the *Times* building. The raucous demonstration was led by Pulitzer-prize-winning colleagues like the *Times'* Eric Nalder.

Next task was signing up for picket duty. If we wanted to collect strike pay, we were expected to contribute 20 hours of picket duty each week. Because I was slow to sign up, I took what was left. My shift would be from 4 a.m. to 8 a.m. at the main *Times* building on Fairview. I was also expected to write a column for the *Union Record*, the strike paper. And, while not initially designated a guild spokeswoman, I inherited the task when *Times* reporter Keiko Morris was called away by a family emergency. One of my early assignments was speaking at service clubs across the region, distributing copies of the *Union Record* and explaining why we were striking. It was not an easy sell to the service club members, most of them businessmen.

Picket duty was a revelation. I reported to my picket station, signed in, and began the downhill-uphill walk around the building, carrying an "On Strike" sign. I quickly discovered that picket stakes are splintery, even while wearing gloves. Next time, I remembered to bring duct tape to cover the raw wood.

Each of the picket stations had a burn barrel, thanks to Boeing union workers who taught us how to tend the fires. The barrels did double duty, both for warmth and for food preparation. You haven't enjoyed breakfast al fresco until you've had an omelet cooked over a burn barrel on a freezing cold morning. Because the region was under a burn ban, it helped that Gov. Gary Locke had declared the burn barrels exempted from the ban. They were designated "religious objects."

Most local politicians sided with the strikers. As a show of support, Seattle Mayor Paul Schell issued an order prohibiting city workers and department heads from granting interviews or providing information to management and replacement employees working at the dailies. Later the mayor was forced to modify his tough stand, allowing replacement workers to attend news conferences. But Schell continued to maintain his personal position: No interviews with scabs.

The strike brought about a 180-degree attitude change. The union cast the family-owned, locally-based *Times* as the devil. The *P-I*'s parent company, the giant Hearst Corporation—once known as labor's archenemy—was portrayed as the more compromising partner. Workers focused on the contrast between unyielding *Times* publisher Frank Blethen, who wrote threatening letters to striking employees saying "come back or else," and the more mellow seeming *P-I* publisher Roger Oglesby.

Fireworks began on the fourth day of the strike when the *Union Record* put out the first hard-copy edition of the strike paper. Peter Horvitz, publisher of the *Eastside Journal*, had agreed to print the hard copy. News of Horvitz's complicity, perceived as disloyal to fellow publishers, infuriated Frank Blethen. Frank responded with a vitriolic email to Horvitz that, once it leaked out, appeared everywhere on the internet. It wasn't only Blethen's strike paper tantrum that fueled strikers' taunts. His past also returned to haunt him. Strikers recalled a May 1996 incident when the publisher became involved in an ugly neighborhood dispute. "Red," a neighbor's Labrador retriever, strayed onto Blethen's Mercer Island property and began chasing the publisher's cats. When Red returned home, the dog's owner, a local attorney, discovered the dog had been shot and was bleeding from a fresh wound to his leg.

Blethen dismissed the incident, referring to it jokingly as "Doggate." He told *Eastside Week* reporters that he had merely aimed a pellet gun at the ground to chase the dog away. He made light of his neighbor's complaint. But the incident was not likely to go away quietly. Animal rights activists marched outside the *Times* building and were featured on the evening TV news. Blethen was charged with a misdemeanor cruelty to animals, ordered to pay Red's vet bills, and sentenced to 20 hours of community service.

No one was surprised when the unionists decided to resurrect the Doggate episode. Striking employees were picketing the *Times* main building, some while leading their canine companions. More than one pooch walked the picket lines wearing a sign that read: "Don't shoot me, Frank."

By the time the strike entered its second week, the opposing parties were still not communicating. Striking workers had put an end to negotiations on November 21 when they rejected the papers' last offer, left the bargaining table, and went on strike.

Matters grew increasingly hostile. At first picketing strikers waved cheerily to their former co-workers, management employees who were crossing picket lines. Those employees were given no option except to quit, which a couple of them did. Management employees were pressed into work, laboring 12-hour days to put out a slimmed-down newspaper.

With attitudes hardening, there were nasty incidents. Mary Rothschild, a line editor who previously had been hugged by strikers when she showed up for work, reported being yelled at, spit upon, and insulted.

As one of the early morning picketers, I was assigned to walk back and forth across John Street at the entrance to the company's executive parking lot. The idea was to obstruct editors and managers who were waiting to enter and park their cars. We kept enforced delays to a two-minute wait, a tactic that, nevertheless, caused backups and raw nerves.

Among those kept waiting was Carol Pucci, a travel writer who had chosen not to join the union. (A provision in the union contract allowed a small percentage of opt-outs.) We watched as Pucci glared and leaned on her horn. Finally parked, she emerged from her car and stomped past the picketers. Within days, the *Times* went to court for an injunction and picketers were restricted to no more than a 45-second delay, even though we were walking on a city sidewalk.

We tried to make the best of a messy situation. As the weather turned still colder, the wind-driven rain was flecked with snowflakes. We warmed ourselves doing "striker aerobics" in front of the *Times* building. We were led by Paula Bock, a tall, agile reporter with aerobics talent. We chanted slogans: "What do we want? Decent wages. When do we want them—NOW!" To keep warm, we twirled our strike signs, band-leader style. We looked something less than a chorus line in our Gore-Tex jackets, rain togs, and water-repellant, tailored garbage bags.

Two weeks into the strike, the opposing sides finally began taking their stories to the public. At a union membership meeting Saturday, December 2, the guild's leaders announced a publicity campaign scheduled to appear in local newspapers and on radio stations. The next day the *Times* Sunday paper fired back with columns authored by *Times* editors and a full-page ad outlining why the guild's strike lacked validity.

Editorial page editor Mindy Cameron wrote a column belittling the strike. She said, "The real story is that this strike, which has turned upside-down the lives of newspaper reporters in this town, is barely a blip in the life of the community we serve."

In his column, Executive Editor Michael Fancher called the guild's request that readers boycott the paper "the ultimate in self-defeating tactics, reminiscent of the Vietnam era notion of destroying a village to save it."

Asked for a response to Fancher's charge, Newspaper Guild spokesman Art Thiel, a *P-I* sports columnist, said, "Obviously economic pressure has to be brought to draw the newspapers to the table. Upon a settlement, the guild and its members are committed to rebuilding circulation as soon as possible."

As the strike entered its third week, guild spokespersons held a press conference at the Pike Place Market. Our little group included Art Thiel, *P-I* cartoonist David Horsey, *Times* sports columnist Ron Judd, and me. We called for a return to the bargaining table. Thiel said, "All we're saying is give talks a chance." He added, "Everything's negotiable," referring to the guild's final proposal.

The Newspaper Guild had proposed wage increases at the *Times* of approximately $3.25 an hour spread over three years, while the *Times* had offered 55 cents over six years. The guild wanted an end to the two-tier wage structure in which suburban employees, reporters, and photographers were paid 15 percent less than Seattle workers. At the *P-I*, the guild was seeking changes to the pension plan and an increase in the number of employees who would be required to join the guild.

Talks resumed early in December. But after five frustrating hours, negotiations broke off again. Bruce Meachum, the guild's chief local negotiator, said the sides were no closer than when the weekend talks began. Both sides blamed the other for the failure, although the management proposal was essentially the same one that the guild had been offered six months previously.

At a December 11 news conference, the guild announced it would more actively promote the circulation and advertising boycott, upping pressure on both papers.

Meanwhile union members complained they were receiving calls from newspaper managers warning that if they didn't return to work immediately, they would be permanently replaced. *Times* managers denied making such calls.

Days earlier, Managing Editor Alex MacLeod had called a number of us to say, "Come back tonight by 11:30 p.m. or don't expect to come back until after the strike is settled." It was a chilling message, particularly since there was so much uncertainty over the possible duration of a strike. During the Detroit newspaper strike, workers were out for 20 months and final resolution had dragged on for five long years.

In Seattle opposing parties continued to disagree on the dimensions of the strike, including details such as the number of workers involved. In a Sunday ad, the *Times* said "over half the *Seattle Times* union-affiliated employees are on the job."

At the Newspaper Guild, statistics showed a different story. The guild said 90 percent of that union's membership were respecting the picket line. Reason for differing numbers? The *Times* was counting workers of craft unions that had already settled. At the eleventh hour, just hours before the guild's strike, Jon Rabine, the all-powerful Teamster boss, had engineered a settlement for one of his unions. It was a back story that begged to be told. The only medium willing to delve into the underlying causes was the *Union Record*, the guild's strike paper.

In the strike's early weeks, the *Union Record* had been doing a professional job, covering both local and national news with only brief articles devoted to the progress of the strike. There had been plenty of hard news for the *Record* to report, including riots marking the first anniversary of Seattle's World Trade Organization battle, the dispute over that year's unsettled presidential election (George W. Bush versus Al Gore), and the much-heralded arrival of Japanese baseball star Ichiro Suzuki to play for the Seattle Mariners.

However, the *Union Record*'s finest hour came in the late weeks of December, a lengthy but highly readable report, headlined: "Anatomy of a Strike." It was authored by three investigative reporters—Susan Kelleher, Eli Sanders, and Stanley Holmes—who looked into the mystery of how and why the strike had occurred.

The story was a complicated one, but clearly one that begged to be told. It revealed a tangled web of assumptions, misunderstandings, and behind-the-scenes double-dealing.

Key to the back story was something called "pattern bargaining." It works this way: A company with multiple unions picks one union to settle with first, preferably a large one with complacent membership. The company gets that union to accept a settlement and then pressures all other unions to accept similar terms.

The *Times* company, responsible for all business functions for the two newspapers, was charged with negotiating contracts with 15 units in seven unions. Since the joint process began in 1983, the *Times* typically set the "pattern," bargaining with either the Pacific Northwest Newspaper Guild or the smaller Teamsters Local 763.

Teamsters' Local 763 represented 572 workers, divided into five bargaining units. Among them were the drivers who distributed newspapers and the machine operators who stuffed advertising supplements into those papers. They were vital links in the chain. As leader of that union, Jon Rabine was the single most important labor representative in contract negotiations. It was he who set the pay pattern for the newspapers during a previous labor action, back in 1987. The Newspaper Guild had been prepared to strike but pulled back after Rabine refused to support the guild. At the time, guild members felt they had been stabbed in the back and the memory still rankled.

Once again, it was Rabine who set the pay pattern. In initial negotiations, he got a basic wage increase of $3.30 over six years for his van drivers and suburban representatives.

At the same time, the guild, which had been negotiating since July, made symbolic requests that went as high as $7.50 an hour, far in excess of what Rabine had achieved. The *Times* termed that proposal "unrealistic." The guild countered, persuading its members to vote a strike authorization back in October, a tactical move designed to increase pressure on the company.

Still the *Times* put off making specific money offers to the guild, continuing to count on pattern bargaining. And, because there hadn't been a strike since 1953, the newspapers assumed that things would not be any different this time.

What Rabine did November 17 was Machiavellian, spurring criticism even among his own union members. After having met dozens of times with the company, he set midnight that night as the deadline for a mailers' strike. The guild deadline was set for three nights later.

In the final hours, Rabine dismissed his bargaining team and met personally with just Jim Schafer, the *Times* chief negotiator, and the federal mediator. Then he called a night meeting of the mailers and distributed incomplete copies of a proposed contract. With only two hours remaining, the mailers rejected the contract 85 to 56. That surprise rejection prompted Rabine to tell members they were on strike.

But within hours union leaders pulled a fast one. They called workers saying the strike had been called off and they should come to work after all. Working overtime, the mailers inserted pages of ads, meant for the day-after Thanksgiving issues, into the prior Monday edition instead. That action, jumping the gun, was a direct hit on the guild, which had set its strike deadline counting on pressure during the holiday, beginning of the newspapers' most lucrative season.

Rabine then resorted to another stunt. He instructed the mailers' foreman to obtain signatures on a "Petition to Settle Contract," a single sheet that gave leaders sole power to settle. What Rabine obtained in those final hours was unprecedented concessions for his union, including front-loaded wage increases, a guarantee of double time-and-a-half for holiday work and a retroactive pay bonus of $2,300 for each worker. What the *Times* management got in return was assurance that the newspapers could continue to publish without the guild.

It was a sweetheart deal, a backstabbing handshake that struck at the heart of the Pacific Northwest Newspaper Guild. Rabine essentially had thrown the guild under a bus driven by his smaller union.

That sleazy settlement was what led *Times* management to believe that it had the upper hand and that the guild would have to be satisfied with less costly gains. As the *Union Record* reporters concluded, "While Rabine points with pride to his contracts, the *Times* and the guild remain on opposite sides of the chain-link fence."

Rabine, arguably Seattle's most powerful union leader, was using the mailers' settlement to boost his own campaign for reelection to head Local 763 and retain his posts as head of the Teamsters' Joint

Council and as vice president of the Teamsters' International. At the same time, Rabine's position at Local 763 was being challenged by a group of reformers battling the leadership system. Despite his crafty backroom deal with the *Times*, Rabine was destined to lose his reelection bid in coming weeks, and, with it, a good deal of his power as a boss of bosses.

Meanwhile, the guild strike continued. As the days stretched on, angst grew in the ranks. With Christmas approaching, it was harder and harder to maintain morale. Some strikers, beset financially and conflicted by divided loyalties, were persuaded to cross picket lines and return to work. As we strikers picketed and paid visits to strike headquarters, rumors circulated. Talk was about who had returned to work and why. We also speculated on possible back stories.

Had the Blethen family changed its mind about never selling the company? What about a rumored deal to sell the *Times* to Knight Ridder Co., the nation's second-largest media company? Knight Ridder had long owned a minority share (49.5 percent) in the *Times*, picked up cheaply during the Depression. One of the unverified stories we heard on the picket line was that CEO Tony Ridder had offered $650 million for the remaining 50.5 percent of the *Times*.

Asked about the offer, Ridder admitted his company was seriously interested in buying the *Times* although he scoffed at the $650 million figure as "seriously overstated." On the picket lines, we heard gossipy stories that Frank Blethen had forced the strike to break the union and thus get a richer offer from Ridder. When asked about those aspects of the story, *Times* spokeswoman Kerry Coughlin refused to disclose the size of the Ridder offer. She insisted, "The Blethens are not interested in selling."

Six days before Christmas, the *Times* sent letters to striking employees informing them that the paper would begin hiring permanent workers to replace the striking staffers. The guild termed the move "illegal" and filed a complaint of unfair labor practices with the National Labor Relations Board. At issue were the harassing calls made to striking employees. The *Times* countered with charges that the guild had broken a promise to take the *Times'* latest offer, essentially the same as the pre-strike offer, to a vote of the membership.

The overall mood had grown far more hostile, evidenced by *Times* President H. Mason Sizemore's remarks at a Tuesday, December 20, news conference. He said, "We will go on without the Guild. We're going to rebuild this company with the folks who want to work for us."

Hearst, the smaller JOA partner with only 130 striking newsroom and business department employees, took a different tack. That company made a new offer, one with fewer paid holidays but with better health-care premiums. Promised that they'd get their old jobs back, *P-I* workers voted to settle on December 28. They returned to work on January 2, all of them at once, marching behind a bagpiper.

At the *Times*, there was a bleaker story to tell. Guild employees voted 399 to 393 to continue the strike. Rallying at the *Times* main building, the strikers called, "We're still here, Frank." To the omnipresent guards they yelled, "Film this!"

By that time Richard Barnes, the Clinton administration's top federal mediator, had been called in. Barnes instituted talks and initially claimed some movement. But credit for the final breakthrough must go to Washington Sen. Patty Murray. Fearing loss of one or the other of her hometown papers, she intervened late in December and summoned Barnes, Blethen, Sizemore, and union leaders to her office in Washington, DC. Patty kept the group talking throughout the night of January 3, personally fetching coffee and sandwiches.

On January 4, 2001, they announced a tentative deal with concessions from both sides. In addition to other details, the guild won phased-in wage increases and the promise that within six months all its members would be back at their jobs. Workers hired as replacements would be removed and assigned elsewhere. After a weekend vote on a contract, the first wave of strikers started returning to work on January 9. It was 49 days—seven weeks—since the strike began.

However for some of us the return to work was slower paced. Since I had been a spokeswoman, I paid for that decision with four more weeks of uncertainty, waiting for a call from management. When I got the call at last, I was instructed to return for my "reeducation," something I'd heard about from my colleagues. I now got to experience reeducation first hand.

On reentering the *Times* building, I was assigned to meet with Managing Editor Suki Dardarian who told me what would be expected of me. She said that I was to continue to write a column, but to confine my columns to people-oriented items. I was not to write about single issues. The column would appear Monday, Wednesday, and Friday and I would no longer have a Sunday column. That was a hurtful blow, since the Sunday paper netted twice the readership of weekdays. The coveted Sunday column space had been given to another columnist, Nicole Brodeur, who crossed the picket line weeks ahead of the settlement.

Oh, and one other thing. Dardarian said that I must never use the word "scab" nor any other derisive word or term in referring to replacement workers or colleagues who crossed the picket line. I was told that would be a firing offense—instantly. The only thing that wasn't mentioned was an admonition against thinking rebellious thoughts.

The strike had finally come to a close. But its lingering effects would be with us for months and years ahead. All the parties had been hurt, fiscally and psychologically. To recoup financial losses, estimated at $13 million in lost ad revenues and $19 million in direct expenses, the *Times* set about cutting several hundred jobs. The cuts, per agreement with the Newspaper Guild, did honor seniority and were achieved mainly through attrition, early-retirement buyouts, and severance packages.

The guild, never a strong force in the region, was weakened and would achieve few gains in the future. And, of course, the striking workers would spend many years recouping personal financial losses. It was a dispute no one had won.

The strike's timing, given changing times and technology, turned out to be almost ruinous. The newspaper industry was looking at a bleak future. Retailers were reporting miserable sales. Dot-com start-ups were failing and high-tech stocks were tanking. The Enron energy crisis gripped the region, causing energy prices to shoot up steeply. The Boeing Company, the region's powerhouse, abruptly announced it was moving its headquarters to Chicago.

At the *Times*, Frank Blethen, still miffed over Mayor Schell's refusal to talk to replacement reporters during the strike, threatened to move the newspaper's headquarters to the suburbs if City Hall didn't change what he viewed as its "anti-business stance."

Were there gains from the strike? There were some, although mostly small unquantifiable gains. There was the solidarity achieved between competing newspaper staffs and between different departments.

In a column appearing in the last edition of the *Seattle Union Record* January 10, Sherry Grindeland, co-chair of the strike's steering committee, celebrated accomplishments, including establishing a solid strike paper virtually overnight that regularly scooped other media. Grindeland had poignant memories. She reported on the day when one woman striker, a single mom, proudly displayed her $300 strike paycheck and told her, "This is more money than I used to bring home from the *Seattle Times*." Grindeland wrote, "I had to go to the restroom to cry."

And, in the end, Seattle still had two daily newspapers, although, sadly, that would not last beyond March 17, 2009, when the *P-I* printed a last edition. The *Times*, although reduced from its pre-strike days, was still able to achieve national notice and well-deserved fame for its superior investigative reporting, adding to its stash of Pulitzer prizes.

For myself, I had finally returned to work without a Sunday column and without as much freedom to write about my beloved city. I had to be content with a slightly larger paycheck and a reduced workload. The strike's conclusion was bittersweet. For many of us, those of us who had so loved our jobs, newspapering would never be quite the same.

11

The Newspaper Wars:
Who Won? 1981–2009

It was just another *Post-Intelligencer* staff meeting on that long-ago afternoon of January 13, 1981. Or so *P-I* staffers foolishly thought.

Reporters, editors and newsroom aides crowded into the *P-I*'s cluttered, paper-strewn newsroom at Sixth and Wall Street. We took in the close-up view of the revolving Elephant Car Wash sign and exchanged educated guesses and gloomy predictions about what might be ahead.

Recent staff meetings had focused on more belt-tightening—finances never being the *P-I*'s strong suit. Or, if the meeting wasn't about layoffs, maybe there would be another upper management shuffle. Maybe it would be like the time when the publisher announced Bill Asbury was taking over as executive editor and former Editor Jack Doughty would take on "long-range projects," *P-I*-speak for "one foot out the door."

We didn't have long to wait. Publisher Virgil Fassio, a tough fire-plug-shaped former University of Pennsylvania grid star, entered the newsroom, his arm in a sling. Attempting to climb onto a desk, he accepted help from a frozen-faced man whom we later learned was a Hearst Corporation lawyer.

Virgil explained the sling, saying he had fallen off a ladder. He then pulled out a paper and read a prepared statement. He announced that Hearst, the *P-I*'s corporate parent, and the *Seattle Times*, the majority owned by the Blethen family, had reached "an agreement in principle." The two papers would enter into a Joint Operating Agreement (JOA). Although the newspapers would remain separate and independent, the *Times* would handle advertising, production, and circulation for both papers.

The *Seattle Times* eagle takes a bite out of the *P-I*'s globe on this T-shirt worn by *Times* staffers. *Author's collection*

The *P-I* would publish six mornings a week; the *Times* in the afternoon, giving up its recent attempt at a morning edition. There would be one joint Sunday edition, with the *P-I* contributing only an editorial section and its syndicated Sunday comics.

Virgil said the *P-I* had lost more than $1 million each year for the last 12 years and that it would take "more than a miracle" to halt the paper's downhill slide. The *P-I*'s losses meant the papers would likely qualify for joint operating status under the Newspaper Act of 1970. That was the bill passed under President Richard Nixon and designed to preserve "failing" newspapers. After throwing the merger bombshell, Virgil curtly stepped down and left, taking no questions.

Astonishing as the news was—and it was volcanic—those of us working on the *P-I*'s editorial pages would have yet another jolt coming. At the time, I was working as assistant editor under Editorial Page Editor Jack de Yonge. We worked to put out the editorial and op-ed pages with editorial writer Nancy Hevly, columnist Shelby Scates, and cartoonist David Horsey.

De Yonge, an Alaska native, explained that the timing of Virgil's news worked for him, as he had been preparing to leave the paper. He told us he had been chosen to take the lead on a study re-examining Alaskan statehood. Would Alaska be better off seceding or not? For Jack, it was a career coup. But, at a precarious time, it left the *P-I* without a chief editorial writer and with me as acting editor.

The news of the newspapers' shot-gun marriage, details still to come, was greeted with astonishment and anger by staff at both papers. *P-I* staffers termed it "V-T Day"—short for "Victory for the *Times*." Especially gut-churning to *P-I* reporters was the decision to give up their Sunday paper.

There was also distress at the *Times*. The newspaper's editors and managers, including then-Circulation Manager Frank Blethen, had worked hard putting out and promoting a single copy morning edition. They felt sold out. They hated being restricted to afternoon publication, losing a shot at the increasingly important morning market. The *P-I* had never been shy about owning Seattle's morning market. During one circulation war, the *P-I*'s delivery staff wore blatantly sexist T-shirts. Their message: "*P-I* Men Do It in the Morning."

Needless to say, the JOA was not universally popular. Over the next two years, JOA opponents—*P-I* reporters, suburban publishers, the Newspaper Guild, and concerned citizens—fiercely fought the agreement. Organized as the "Committee for an Independent P-I," they found a champion in William Dwyer, one of the nation's best trial lawyers. Amazingly, Dwyer took on the case pro bono. The opposition feared that the JOA would silence diverse voices while simultaneously giving the *Times* monopoly power over advertising rates.

Opponents argued the *P-I* was not really a failing paper. They claimed Hearst's losses were merely the result of creative bookkeeping. They cited inflated amounts Hearst charged the *P-I* for syndicated columns and editorial cartoons (most discarded as useless or far too clunky). The *P-I* paid dearly for such "must runs" as a Sunday column written by—some said "ghost written" for—Hearst Publisher William Randolph Hearst Jr. Each August, Junior's column marked his father's passing with a repeat of Hearst Sr.'s poem "Song of the River."

For the sloppy sentimental poem and for other Hearst features, the *P-I* was assessed millions.

With its headquarters located in New York City, the Hearst Corporation had seldom paid much attention to its Seattle paper. Hearst execs considered the *P-I* little more than a suburban bureau of the *San Francisco Examiner*, the company's flagship. So little was known about Seattle on the other coast that, during the 1964 Anchorage earthquake, Hearst executives in New York told the *P-I* editor to dispatch reporters to cover the story "never mind expenses—by cab if necessary."

Objections to federal approval of the JOA were many. Some opponents argued this way: If Hearst had sold the *P-I*, some other owner could have made the paper profitable. In fact, during the two years of contested JOA legalities, opponents tried to interest other publishers. Prospects included the *New York Times*, the *Wall Street Journal*, and even publishing magnate Rupert Murdoch.

One *P-I* staffer, Washington, DC, reporter Solveig Torvik, took advantage of an encounter at the annual White House Correspondents' Dinner to urge *Washington Post* owner Katherine Graham to purchase the *P-I*. We heard frequent rumors about other prospective buyers. Among the tamer ones was television commentator Bill Moyers. But that rumor, like all the others, came to nothing.

Although sympathetic to the cause, I was unable to stand with the JOA's visible opponents. As acting editorial page editor during the next contentious months (and, by the way, paid far less than my male predecessor's salary), I faced having to meet each morning with the publisher and did not have the luxury of opposition. During my time supervising the *P-I*'s editorial pages, I often fielded phone calls from Virgil Fassio insisting that we pull anything that looked remotely anti-business, anti-merger, or even anti-Mariners baseball. I often had to defend the cartoons of David Horsey, the newspaper's resident cartoonist, who sometimes veered awfully close to lampooning business.

Meanwhile, I silently cheered early opposition wins. At first there was the decision by the Department of Justice's Antitrust Division rejecting the JOA application since there appeared to be prospective buyers for the "failing" paper. However, those hopes were soon dashed. U.S. Attorney General William French Smith ruled that the failing newspaper test did not require the presence or absence of willing buyers.

The Committee for an Independent P-I next went to court and won a favorable ruling from U.S. District Judge Barbara Rothstein. She ruled that there could be no JOA without exploring other alternatives. Opponents barely had time to celebrate when, on an appeal, the Ninth Circuit Court overturned Judge Rothstein's decision.

After many days spent in courtrooms, the two newspapers finally got the go-ahead for their agreement. The decision came down despite damning testimony about ineffective Hearst management, detailed by former *P-I* editors Bill Asbury and Lou Guzzo. Nevertheless, the circuit court decision prevailed, allowing the papers to combine production, delivery, advertising, circulation, and marketing. The *Times* would manage those operations and, after expenses, would receive two-thirds of the profits.

Within days, the deed was done. In the early hours of May 29, 1983, the noisy, building-shaking presses at Sixth and Wall fell forever silent. The first joint Sunday paper, a 292-page "Super Sunday" package carried the flags of both newspapers. But the Sunday edition was, of course, published by the *Times*. Folded inside, close to the back of the package, was the *P-I's* anemic six-page "Focus" section, along with a combined crop of Sunday comics.

In the early months and years of the JOA, the arrangement seemed to be working. There were circulation gains at both papers. Both publishers attested to the merger's success. And, incredibly, the *Times* still led in circulation, an anomaly in a nation where afternoon papers were dying.

For both papers, there were changes ahead. At the *Times*, editors convinced Publisher Jerry Pennington, principal architect of the merger, that the company would have to invest a large share of its JOA profits in the newsroom. It was that or the publisher could forget his often-stated goal of becoming one of the top U.S. papers.

Just as the *Times* started to realize the benefits of beefed-up news-room resources, word came of an untimely accident. The 66-year-old Pennington drowned while setting out crab pots at his Whid-bey Island home. Days later on March 18, 1985, Frank Blethen, by then vice president of sales and marketing, assumed a new role. He became the newspaper's new CEO, a Blethen Corporation director, and the *Seattle Times*' seventh publisher.

There were also major changes at the *P-I*. During the lengthy JOA negotiations, Hearst executives decided the paper badly needed updating, a complete typographical make-over. They hired Austra-lian media consultant Ted Bolwell, who came recommended to the Hearsts by a fellow newspaper giant, Rupert Murdoch.

Bolwell's make-over resulted in a series of dubious design changes. He insisted on rigid style and layout formats. He was also responsi-ble for hiring two new editors, James Rennie from the *Ottawa Jour-nal* and John Reistrup, a former *Washington Post* newsman. It was a power struggle waiting to happen.

Winner of the clash was Rennie, who forcefully took over as managing editor, supervising news, sports, business, and photogra-phy. That left Reistrup to assume the title of "executive editor" and to oversee the newspaper's feature sections, the editorial page, and the soon-to-be-axed Sunday *P-I*.

Rennie, a hard-nosed newsman and reformed alcoholic, immedi-ately became known for his hair-trigger temper. He directed scream-ing tirades at both reporters and editors. In the newsroom, we called them Rennie's "nut outs." He seemed unable to control his tantrums, although we noticed that he was far more profane reprimanding male employees than in dressing down women. On at least one occasion, he resorted to actual physical attack, whacking reporter Don Carter on the arm and shoulder with a rolled-up newspaper.

I was witness to several of the editor's outbursts. The first occurred in 1982 when I was hastily summoned to Rennie's office. At the time, I was the paper's business editor, a job I assumed after a year as acting editorial page editor. Rennie abruptly kicked the door shut and began loudly berating me. He was angry over my down-page treatment of a speech given by beer magnate Bill Coors to Rotary Number Four, Seattle's big downtown chapter.

"You don't know news when you see it!" Rennie thundered. Instead of featuring Coors' anti-union diatribe as the day's lead, I had bannered a story about upscale businesses moving into the new Pacific Place development. For my sin, Rennie sentenced me to attend a day-long management class. One of the first subjects at the class: "How to Handle an Electric Boss."

On another occasion, I was one of several editors in the *P-I* bullpen listening to Sunday editor John McCoy's proposals for a feature layout on the city's prosperous gay community, the so-called "A-Gays." Rennie started to perspire heavily and became flushed. A vein in his forehead began throbbing. I began to wonder what would happen if he actually passed out: Would we just let him lie there? Or would we administer CPR? As it happened, the red-faced Rennie growled that he'd think over McCoy's proposal. He slammed into his office, and we never heard about the feature idea again.

The atmosphere at the *P-I* was toxic enough to tempt reporters to seek greener pastures. Soon after the merger, some of the brightest and best were lured to the wealthier and more ambitious *Seattle Times*. Among those who "crossed the street"— a bitter phrase coined by *P-I* publisher Virgil Fassio—were Eric Nalder, Duff Wilson, and Casey Corr. Eventually the list would expand to include Seattle's preeminent columnist, Emmett Watson.

In 1993, on the tenth anniversary of joint operations, the *Times'* Terry McDermott took a look back in a retrospective article. He marked the anniversary, took stock of gains and losses, and revisited earlier concerns. He scored as overrated the JOA opponents' worries about the silencing of diverse voices. The two papers often expressed opposite editorial opinions. Both papers carried a range of reader comments and op-ed columns, local and national.

McDermott even examined the pre-JOA rumor that the *P-I* globe, the newspaper's iconic neon sign, would be sold. That was an unnecessary worry. In fact, the *P-I* sign was expensively repaired and moved to the paper's new home on the Seattle waterfront. Worries over rising advertising rates also were overblown; the joint papers' advertising rates had not grown markedly more expensive.

On a cautionary note, McDermott pointed out that, during the first JOA decade, combined circulation of the two papers had not increased significantly, nor had circulation kept up with population growth. McDermott darkly noted that "the JOA ignores the dynamics of the information market." He concluded the fate of newspapers probably had less to do with internecine battles "than with what the market does to them."

That said, the city's newspaper battles were not over. There was more to come. Frank Blethen had not gotten over his initial distress over the JOA restricting his paper to afternoon circulation. It was only too clear that few afternoon papers were profitable. Gridlocked traffic already was adversely impacting the *Times'* afternoon delivery. Furthermore, many of the region's newcomers were accustomed to getting their news in the morning. The *Times* still maintained a circulation lead over the *P-I*, but it was apparent that the paper needed to get with the times.

Blethen set to work renegotiating the JOA. In return for giving the *Times* the right to publish in the morning, the *P-I* would get the go-ahead to increase its internet presence and would receive a larger share of the joint profits—upped from 32 percent to 40 percent. Remaining in place was the provision that the Hearst Corporation would continue to receive its share of profits, even if the *P-I* stopped publishing.

The new JOA was extended 50 years, lasting until 2083. On its behalf, the Hearst Corporation insisted upon and received the right of first refusal to buy the *Times* if the Blethen family decided to sell. In return Hearst agreed to pay the Blethens $1 million a year for the next 10 years.

News of the renegotiated JOA led to dire predictions. The *Seattle Weekly*, an alternative paper that had opposed the JOA, called the new deal a "Suicide Pact." *Weekly* publisher David Brewster claimed it set the stage to put one or the other paper, most likely the *P-I*, out of business. Brewster wrote that Hearst could merely "go to the Justice Department with new evidence of being a failing paper, close the *P-I* and clip coupons until 2083."

Reaction to a revised JOA fueled a tsunami of rumors that the *P-I* was for sale. Posted on the *P-I* newsroom's so-called Bitch Board, an employee-run bulletin board positioned above the ever-present coffee urn, were the usual anonymous comments. Under the headline "Top P-I Sale rumors" were the following:

"Hearst entering into a JOA with the Mariners."

"Times wants equal billing on the P-I Globe: 'It's in the *Times/P-I.*'"

"Times wants to buy out the P-I softball team."

"Fancher and MacLeod (editors Mike and Alex) covet P-I's waterfront view."

"P-I to relocate to Yakima [the Blethens owned a paper there] in three-way trade."

University of Washington communications professor and former *Times* reporter Doug Underwood noted that prior to renegotiation the two newspapers had achieved "one of the last successful JOAs in the country." Of the nation's 28 original JOAs only 15 remained. Underwood warned that, under provisions of a reworked JOA, the papers were entering shaky territory.

What the papers really were entering was a battle for Seattle. That conflict began in earnest as the first copies of the morning *Times* touched home doorsteps on March 6, 2000. Although it was sweet for me personally (I had missed being on breakfast tables during my first years at the *Seattle Times*), the switch to morning publication would turn bittersweet.

Hearst prepared for the contest by beefing up staff and appointing a new publisher, the *Los Angeles Times'* Roger Oglesby. But despite boosted resources and its typical feisty approach (the staff wore T-shirts that bragged "First in the Morning"), the *P-I* was steadily losing circulation. Meanwhile at the *Times*, where staffers wore T-shirts that showed the *Times'* Eagle taking a healthy bite from the *P-I* globe, circulation had increased. The *Times'* numbers did improve, but only modestly.

Then a series of disasters struck. First there were the enormous economic losses suffered by both papers during the 2000 Newspaper Guild strike. Following closely on that wrenching blow were impacts from the terrorist attacks of September 11, 2001, and the nationwide recession that followed.

In January 2003 the *Times* announced that it had lost money for three consecutive years and planned to trigger an escape clause that would allow it to dissolve the JOA. Hearst countered saying that, under the *force majeure* provision, losses incurred during the 2000 strike could not be counted. On April 28, 2003, Hearst filed suit in King County Superior Court, alleging that mismanagement by the *Times* had cost the *P-I* millions.

The newpapers' battle for Seattle quickly moved into lawyerland and the two sides clashed in courtrooms over the next three years. Blethen claimed that support given the *P-I* threatened to drain his paper. He complained of being "yoked to the *P-I*" and said Seattle could not sustain two daily papers. The *Puget Sound Business Journal* quoted Blethen saying, "It is not our intent to let the Hearst Corporation bleed one of the few remaining independent papers out of existence."

The *Times* prevailed in two higher court decisions over the question of whether or not the strike losses could be counted in the effort to end the JOA. The *Times* seemed to be winning its case.

And then, to widespread surprise, everyone blinked.

In March 2006, the two owners hastily left the courtroom and announced that they planned to enter confidential, binding arbitration on the future of the JOA and on whether the *P-I* was entitled to damages stemming from alleged mismanagement. The warring parties tapped retired King County Superior Judge Larry Jordan as the arbitrator. He was scheduled to hear the case on April 9, 2007, a date later postponed until April 16. As the hearing date approached, the two parties engaged in intense closed-door negotiations. They reached a settlement with just one day to spare on April 15.

Under the settlement, the *Times* agreed to take no more actions to end the JOA for nine years—at least until 2016. The *Times* also accepted new accounting restrictions limiting expense amounts charged to the joint operation. Hearst, for its part, gave up the right to collect its percentage of the profits should the *P-I* close before JOA expiration. That concession came at a price. After monetary adjustments were made on both sides, the *Times* handed over a net $24 million payment.

That left bystanders to speculate: What had led to the abrupt settlement? Some thought mounting legal expenses played a major role. It was true that in order to pay escalating legal fees, the *Times* had been forced sell its extensive real estate holdings in South Lake Union. The *Times* also sold a parcel of land in Renton, bought for a possible second printing plant. Observers pointed out that, even if the *Times* had somehow "won" its court case, a group called the Committee for a Two-Newspaper Town, granted the right to intervene, could continue litigation and would become a major problem for both papers.

Meanwhile, the warning delivered by reporter Terry McDermott about the changing information market was materializing. The internet was fast becoming the rival of conventional news, absorbing classified ad revenues on which the papers had relied and competing through faster delivery.

At the *P-I*, the settlement was greeted with relief and enthusiasm. Publisher Roger Olgesby called it "a nine-year opportunity." Staffers were especially pleased that the *P-I*'s name would be restored to the *Times'* fleet of delivery trucks.

Announcement of the April 15 settlement led *P-I* staffers to embark on a riotous evening of revelry. A hired limo full of *P-I* reporters ended the evening by relieving themselves directly onto the lawn across from the *Seattle Times* building. The urine-fueled stunt was marked on the *P-I* bitch board as "The Revenge of the Pee-Eye."

While the *P-I* celebrated, the mood at the *Times* was far more subdued. When Dave Boardman, the new executive editor, explained the outcome, staffers asked hard questions. Reporters wanted to know how the *Times* could continue supporting the *P-I*, which it had billed as "a failing paper."

Questions aside, the net response at the *Times,* under Boardman, was a renewed dedication to quality journalism. The editor pushed his slimmed-down staff to do an exceptional job covering the news. While all newspapers across the country were losing value and many were failing, the *Times* countered by winning an impressive share of distinguished awards.

The *P-I*'s reprieve, celebrated so boisterously in 2007, did not last nearly the nine hoped-for years. In fact, the stay of execution spanned slightly less than two years.

On January 9, 2009, Hearst Newspaper President Steven R. Swartz arrived from New York for a morning staff meeting. He confirmed the painful sales rumor, reported on KING-TV the previous evening. Swartz pulled no punches. He simply said, "The *P-I* is for sale." He told the newsroom that, should no buyer could be found in 60 days, the *P-I* was destined to become an internet-only news source with a far smaller staff. Then he refused, Hearst style, to take questions.

It was bitter news, the end of a print *P-I* after a century and a half of survival, years that saw the paper outlast 20 rivals. News of the newspaper's impending demise was greeted sadly but gamely by staffers who continued to put out the paper with show-goes-on bravery for the next two months. On March 16, the publisher told staffers that they would be putting out the final print edition the next morning.

It fell to *Post-Intelligencer* reporter and writing coach Carol Smith, an office mate of mine in years past, to write the print paper's obituary for the next day's commemorative edition. She pulled at all our hearts—even the hearts of opposition newsies—when she wrote,

> Writing obituaries is a rite of passage for journalists—a first beat for cub reporters and often the last for those who have been around long enough to have covered or been friends or enemies with those whose passings they note.
>
> Eventually, a gut-punch of an obit comes along. Now it's our turn. The news of the end, when it finally came, was swift and surgical. Cause of death—a fatal spiral compounded by dwindling subscription rates, an exodus of advertisers and an explosion of on-line information. News will live on. This newspaper will not.

She added what we—those of us who once worked there—knew: "We went down doing what we loved."

On that more-blue-than-green St. Patrick's Day, March 17, 2009, the newspaper war ended, the battle for Seattle was over. The *Seattle Times* had won. Yet, given the economic realities of the news business, it was a somewhat Pyrrhic victory. The *Times* lives on but with much reduced value. A decade ago, Tony Ridder of Knight-Ridder, the minority shareholder, had offered $500 million for a 50.5 percent share of the *Times*. In recent days, the worth of that share has been drastically reduced, valued at $19 million. The staff, too, is far smaller than in pre-strike, pre-JOA days. What hasn't changed, however, is the paper's plucky dedication to keeping a family-owned paper operating and a credit to its community.

Whatever one thinks of the JOA, those who write about the newspaper wars, notably John Hughes in *Pressing On: Two Family-Owned Newspapers in the 21st Century*, believe that the joint operation prolonged the *P-I's* print life by at least 15 years. However, Hughes is quick to conclude, conventional wisdom to the contrary, Frank Blethen did not kill the *P-I*.

Who or what killed the newspaper? Many observers blame the information industry's changing economics. Others—perhaps invested in conspiracy theory—pin the lion's share of guilt directly on the Hearst Corporation. They argue that Hearst was an absentee parent that failed the paper, squandered its morning position, failed to modernize, neglected its assets, and declined to invest in the *P-I's* future. The reasons are still debated in newspaper circles.

As a postscript, there remains one tangible memorial to the *P-I's* rambunctious century and a half. That *memento mori* is the *P-I* globe, the three-story, 13-ton neon sign, all that remains of the newspaper's physical assets. After the print paper closed, three Seattle councilmembers, all former journalists, Sally Clark, Tim Burgess, and I worked to have the globe successfully landmarked. Donated by the Hearsts to the Museum of History and Industry, the sign is scheduled for refurbishing. With luck, the globe will keep memories of the feisty newspaper revolving into the future.

12

Candidate Godden, 2003

When I wrote columns for the *Seattle Times*, the first job each day was sorting through my mail. I checked it all: snail mail, voice mail, and email. There I would find juicy news tips, interesting story ideas, blatant self-promotion, and a slew of other messages—some obscene, many worth a laugh or two.

What looked intriguing among my emails one June morning was a press release from Seattle City Councilmember Judy Nicastro. The release stated that the first-term councilmember had chalked up a record fundraising month in May. She had outraised other council candidates and banked more than $25,000 for her fall reelection campaign.

Twenty-five thousand in a single month was worth writing home about. Council races at that time—it was 2003—cost around $150,000. Nicastro had rounded up a substantial war chest in record time.

The obvious question: Where had she raised that much money, averaging almost a thousand dollars a day? Thanks to public disclosure laws, I could easily check out the names of her contributors on the Seattle Ethics and Elections Commission website.

Who had donated? The names left me stunned. Nicastro was accepting max-out money from the Colacurcio family, owners of a string of nude dance clubs that included Rick's, the infamous, windowless topless club in Lake City. She not only was accepting Colacurcio money, but she had picked up a contribution from Roger Forbes, owner of a competing strip club. She had also taken in money from owners of naked dance clubs as far afield as Texas.

How could Nicastro take money—much less brag about it—from the Colacurcios? Was it ignorance or naivety? Frank Colacurcio and his son Frank Jr. were well known locally for shady dealings. In the past, Frank Sr. had been accused of profit skimming, tax fraud, and fostering prostitution. He had served prison terms for racketeering

This is How Jean Godden Sees Ethics.

To Jean Godden ethics are a black and white issue.

Secret meetings, land use votes to accommodate a strip club, illegal contributions, Seattle Ethics & Elections Commission violations and fines, donations returned to strip club owners, vote-trading and back-room deals.

These headlines have had a devastating effect on the public trust in government.

Jean Godden is running for Seattle City Council to make ethics a part of our city council again. Jean has been a journalist for over 20 years – a profession that depends on knowing and respecting ethical boundaries. As an editorial writer, business editor and reporter, Jean is known for her integrity, balance and objectivity. A former board member of the League of Women Voters of Seattle, Jean Godden understands the need for ethics in the leaders we elect.

Perception is reality when it comes to the public's trust.

Judy Nicastro did not see the ethical implications of taking thousands of dollars in contributions from strip club proponents, then voting for the zoning change they wanted. That's the most troubling point of all. She never understood the public's outrage over her behavior.

Giving the money back is not the solution; rescinding the land use vote is not the solution.

Electing people with ethics you can trust: That's the solution.

Let's rebuild the trust.

Elect Jean Godden
Seattle City Council, Pos. 1

Paid for by Friends of Jean Godden • P.O. Box 21522 • Seattle, WA 98111

This 2003 campaign postcard explains why I decided to run for Seattle City Council. *Author's collection* in 1971 and tax fraud in 1981. He had connections to Salvatore "Bill" Bonanno, son of New York Mafia boss Joseph ("Joe Bananas") Bonanno.

After reading about Nicastro's shady contributors, I pointed out the names to a *Seattle Times* colleague, police reporter Steve Miletich. Steve made the same connection and later wrote about Nicastro's generous but dubious donors. Others in the media did so as well. Among the first to break the story in print was *Seattle Sun* reporter James Bush.

In the meantime, Nicastro, who chaired the city council's land use committee, had persuaded fellow councilmembers to approve a rezone that Rick's had been seeking for many years. Approved in June 2003 by a 5 to 4 vote of the council, legislation allowed the strip club to expand, extending its rear parking lot into a single-family residential zone.

Nicastro had banked money for her campaign and then—in what looked like a quid pro quo—she had handed the Colacurcios that disputed spot rezone. Questionable contributions totaling $36,000 went to three councilmembers, but Nicastro collected the lion's share, around $20,000.

Expanding the strip club parking lot meant more spaces for employee parking. It also made room for motor homes and vans that parked in back of the club and sometimes even spilled over into the adjacent Bigfoot Car Wash lot. Given the club's erotic activities, lap dances plus a condom machine in the men's room, one didn't need much imagination to guess what might be taking place.

News media followed the story and began using the term "Strippergate" to describe the possible connection between campaign contributions and the rezone. When asked about the seeming ethical lapse, Nicastro, a New Jersey native, at first was dismissive. She was quoted in the *New York Times*, August 27, 2003, saying, "It looks like a bad episode of 'The Sopranos.'"

She implied that people in Seattle were over-reacting. "Seattle's nothing but Mayberry with high rises," she said.

The discovery of Nicastro's situational ethics left me kicking myself. Like many a reporter who covered city government, I often fantasized that I could do a better job than those in office. But I probably had waited too long and grown too senior—put less politely: too old. If elected office had been my goal, I should have thought of it years ago. The deadline for filing for city offices was only weeks away. Forget it, I thought.

Still the idea of running for office kept haunting me, sometimes in the wee hours of the night. It is true I loved my job writing about the city and its residents. But ever since the newspaper strike and the loss of my Sunday column, life as a city scribe was not as sweet as it once had been. Besides, the newspaper, drained of much ad revenue by online sites, was not the place it had been. I was in a quandary.

By coincidence, I was having dinner with a few friends later that month, and one of the guests was political consultant Cathy Allen. Her job was to help candidates run for office. Minorities and women candidates were her specialty. I posed a crazy question to her: If I quit my job to run against Nicastro—something I would have to do in order to seek office—did I stand a chance?

Although my dinner guests were encouraging, I continued to harbor grave doubts. They, like most of my friends and acquaintances, worked in the media and would be no help. They couldn't ethically take a political stand. They couldn't support me, couldn't contribute to a campaign or even work behind the scenes. In fact, if I ran, given the strict ethics of professional journalists, they would have to stay at arm's length.

Allen thoughtfully considered my pipe dream and said, "I could do an overnight survey. It'll cost you—around $4,000—but it would be money well spent. It would tell you whether you'd have an outside chance."

Several weeks later, Allen arranged the poll and called me one evening in late July to report that, yes, my chances were pretty good. My positives were four times the positives of the incumbent councilmember. Because of my years as a daily columnist, the people surveyed thought they knew me and, to believe the numbers, they even liked me.

The next day was the final day to file for elective office. I would have to make a decision overnight. I slept better than I thought I would and the next morning wakened at 5:30 a.m.

Crazy or not, I decided to go for it. I sat down at my home laptop and wrote a letter to Executive Editor Dave Boardman resigning my job after 12 years at the *Seattle Times*. And there I was, 71 years old, leaving arguably the best job in the world, with no assurance I could be elected.

At 9 a.m., I delivered my letter of resignation to Boardman. He wished me luck and then he said, "Don't expect any favors. We will cover you like any other candidate." It was harsh, but true, and no more than I had expected. We bid farewell with a friendly hug. I handed over my ID and said goodbye to reporters in the "dead zone," the corner of the city room where I wrote my columns. I was told I could return later to pick up my personal effects, supervised by security guards.

And then, accompanied by Allen, I walked from her office on Stewart to the King County elections office. There I wrote the required $850 check and filed for Position One, the Nicastro seat, on the Seattle City Council.

To be honest, I felt strangely light-headed and disoriented. For the first time in 29 years, I was solidly on the other side of the notebook. Even though I'd covered many candidates and elections, I had no idea what it took to manage a campaign or how to raise money. I didn't even know what to say if asked about my late-in-life decision.

First task was to find a campaign manager. Allen suggested her co-worker Tom Van Bronkhorst. I had run into Tom in 2001 when I travelled to Casablanca with Allen and others. We were there helping Moroccan women run for office. My volunteer task in Morocco: Tell the would-be candidates how to handle the press. In other words, "Take a reporter to lunch."

Now I was the one who desperately needed help, and I would need to find a campaign manager, someone who knew the ropes. Yet when Tom and I sat down to talk, it felt as if I were being interviewed rather than the other way around.

Tom asked tough questions, ones I was sure to be asked: Why was I running? What did I hope to accomplish? Was there anything embarrassing in my background? And what would I say when people accused me of being nothing but "a washed-up gossip columnist?"

To the last question, I replied that it wouldn't be the first time I'd heard the "G word." Gossip, I had learned, is an old English word that means "between cousins." I had approached writing a column as if chatting with a neighbor—or cousin perhaps—over the back fence. Besides, the "G word" is arguably sexist. I have yet to hear of a male columnist, no matter how people-oriented, being called "a gossip columnist."

Must have been the right answer because next I was off with my campaign manager to get a new cell phone, one with unlimited minutes to use while campaigning.

That was hardly the only change in my life. Allen, acting as my campaign consultant, recruited Tamara Wilson, a style-conscious PR friend, to go home with me and clean out my closet: No more newspaper casual. I would have to dress for the campaign. A half-dozen pairs of my shoes were shipped off to the shoemaker for half soles and polishing. By the time Wilson finished sorting, there was a three-foot pile of discards for Goodwill. Right on top were my well-worn Cole Hahn loafers and, cruelest cut of all, my vintage trench coat.

Next assignment: a trip to buy clothing fit for a candidate. "Keep it under $1,000," Allen said. Wilson promptly turned a deaf ear; her good taste managed to severely dent my Nordstrom card. On the plus side, I had a wardrobe fit for fundraisers, interviews, and candidate forums.

All that was missing from the picture was the right haircut, a task left to Roberto, a professional stylist who had clients from both sides of the aisle, among them Sen. Maria Cantwell and Rep. Dave Reichert. On Sunday afternoons, Roberto opened his Third Avenue shop exclusively for then Gov. Gary Locke and First Lady Mona Locke.

If my new look—clothing and hairstyle—was important, even more critical was improving my speaking skills. Although I could write, I knew I was no public speaker. I would need to deliver a two-minute speech about why I was running and I had better give it my best shot.

Lorraine Howell came to the rescue. Howell had been a TV producer and now taught public speaking. She arrived with her compact TV camera, conducted mock interviews, and played back the results for a cringe-making critique. We rehearsed for hours. At one point, Howell had me lying face-up on the floor, delivering my speech, and projecting my voice towards the ceiling.

Soon after, I had my first interview as a candidate. I found myself explaining my decision to a *Seattle Weekly* reporter who met me on a plaza outside Allen's office. In the background, Howell was watching to assess my skills. It was the beginning of a steep learning curve.

On Monday, August 4, my first day on the new "job," my campaign manager assigned me a desk in Allen's offices. I was given a phone and an assignment to spend the morning making calls for endorsements and potential financial backing. Difficult as it was to ask for money, it wasn't nearly as hard as telling voters how good I thought I was or why they should support me. Perhaps due to childhood conditioning, I found it hard to toot my own horn.

It took one of my new campaign workers to help me over the money-raising hurdle. Kathleen Durkan, who came from a political family headed by the late Sen. Martin Durkan Sr., had a memorable approach. She spoke forcefully, telling me: "Remember you aren't asking for yourself. You are asking for the campaign. And, if you don't believe in the campaign, you shouldn't be running."

As I eased into campaigning, I soon met Nicastro's other challengers. Damaged by stories about Strippergate, the incumbent Nicastro had drawn five other opponents, all men. They were an interesting lot: Darryl Smith, a Columbia City realtor; David Ferguson, member of the Socialist Alternative party; Kollin Min, an attorney and former aide to state House Speaker Frank Chopp; Art Skolnik, an architect and preservationist; and Robert Rosencrantz, a landlord.

The six of us became friendly at candidate forums, biding our time while waiting for Nicastro, who was invariably late. Position One, the largest city council race, presented logistical headaches.

One night all seven of us debated in the International District, seated on rickety folding chairs and lined up alphabetically. Ironically, Ferguson, the left-leaning socialist, was on the audience's far right with me next in line. Teetering on the edge of the stage, Ferguson started to tumble. The rest of us reacted quickly, grabbing his arms to keep him from falling off the stage and injuring himself. We had grown close enough to talk about holding Position One reunions.

The 2003 campaign highlighted such issues as the Strippergate fiasco, South Lake Union land use changes, soaring City Light bills, a sour economy, and a proposed latte tax slated to appear on the September primary ballot.

As challengers we criticized irrelevant council actions such as an anti-Iraq War resolution that was debated for weeks, reworded, watered down, and not passed until after the actual shooting started. We also targeted a politically naïve resolution calling for removal of dams on the Snake River in Eastern Washington, arguably a good idea, but not an immediate Seattle concern. The dam resolution fueled anger throughout the state and became an excuse, as if one were needed, to oppose anything Seattle wanted from the state legislature.

When I answered questions at forums and interviews, I spoke guardedly. I had a reporter's concern for accuracy and an unfortunate tendency to couch my responses. Finally my campaign manager Tom Van Bronkhorst lectured me on my over-cautious style and said he would charge me 25 cents for every "maybe" or "probably."

After a KOMO-TV forum, a debate that I thought I had handled well, I asked, "How did I do?" Tom sighed, looked pained. He said, "Jean, you don't have enough money in your wallet."

The primary that year, set for Tuesday, September 16, occurred a mere six weeks after I had made the decision to run. Nicastro came in first with 43 percent of the vote, not an ideal number for an incumbent. I finished second, less than 200 votes ahead of Rosencrantz. As election workers counted dozens of absentee ballots, my lead kept slipping: 181 votes ahead, then only 164. It was a nail biter. Yet with the general election only weeks away, I had to keep campaigning. The cliffhanger lasted a tense two weeks. But, finally, all the votes were counted and I had placed second. I had squeaked through the primary with a bare cushion—147 votes.

Now I was left, face to face, with the incumbent and things turned uglier. Allen, my political consultant, was designing a mailer directly targeting Nicastro's ethics. She planned to use what I thought was an exceptionally slutty picture of Nicastro. I said I would think about it, but such negative campaigning seemed wrong to me. It was something I desperately wanted to avoid.

As I was about to say "no way," Tom stepped in and bluntly asked me if I was willing to "let my supporters down." It was a manipulative move, but he had made his point. At the last minute, I gulped and agreed. The day before the negative mailer was due for mailing, a Nicastro mailer arrived in my mailbox. The opposition piece featured an especially unfortunate picture of me. I looked like a deranged bag lady. Somehow my decision on the "ethics" mailer no longer seemed so wrong. We were surprised to learn later that the steamy picture we had used of Judy was a great favorite of hers.

I campaigned hard in the final days, spending every spare moment calling supporters, asking for endorsements and appearing wherever there was a crowd. One sunny noon, I was campaigning at Westlake Center Plaza, shaking hands and introducing myself. I spotted an older woman, maybe within my demographic, drinking coffee and resting beside the Starbucks kiosk.

"Hello," I said brightly. "I'm Jean Godden and I'm running for Seattle City Council."

"Know who you are," replied the woman.

"Hope I can count on your vote," I added.

"Don't think so," she said. "I'm Judy Nicastro's mother."

Later that week, I had to meet Nicastro in a one-on-one debate on the Seattle Channel, the city cable station located at City Hall. I pulled the Green Pea, my old Dodge sedan, into the Sixth Avenue city garage with Tom in the passenger's seat. I stepped out of the car and, because my hands were full, I shoved the driver's door shut with my hip. Ouch! The door slammed shut on my right index finger. I looked back and caught a sickening sight: My finger disappearing into the door jamb.

Was it broken? I froze, scared to look. But, when Tom turned the door handle, the finger, although skinned and bleeding, seemed to be operating. I trailed blood as I walked into City Hall, heading for the restroom to wash it away. Adjacent to the women's room was the Citizen's Service Bureau.

I walked into the bureau and asked if they could help me. A nice man at the counter explained that they weren't trained to perform first aid, but he did offer me a Band-Aid. I thanked him and took it. I wrapped the bandage as tightly as I could with my clumsy left hand and hoped I wouldn't bleed during the debate.

Although hurting, I managed to make points succinctly and answer effectively. Moderator C. R. Douglas quizzed the two of us on a list of city problems—steep City Light bills, traffic snarls, allegations of racial profiling by Seattle police, and the council's preoccupation with issues such as the ban on circus animals and removal of the Snake River dams.

Afterward, Tom, who had been off stage watching, expressed rare approval. He credited the smashed finger with focusing my attention. He jokingly offered to slam my fingers in a car door before future debates. Luckily, it was the last of the close campaign encounters.

The week before the general election, I got a phone call with startling news. Larry Cobb, one of my neighbors, reported that a Seattle Department of Transportation truck transporting a road grader had gotten lost. It strayed into our narrow, dead-end street. When the misguided truck tried to turn around, the grader broke free, careened down the hilly street and smashed right through my garage door. It splintered the door and stopped mere feet from a connecting door into my kitchen.

Cobb, a home builder, said he had a crew working nearby and offered to have the crew board up my garage until things could be sorted out and a new garage door installed. On the good side, no one had been hurt. The only victim was the door. The accident was not, I hoped, a bad omen.

On election night, as the first returns came in, I was standing at a podium at the Pyramid Alehouse across from Safeco Field, my election night party venue. I was doing my best to look presentable and deliver an upbeat message. It was early, but so far I had captured 53 percent of the first returns. As I glanced at my notes, I looked down at the lectern. There, staring me in the face, was a large "Vote for Judy" sticker, enough to disrupt one's train of thought. I had no doubt that it was the work of a reporter from *The Stranger*, the alternative paper that had endorsed my opponent.

The second and last returns of the night seemed to confirm that I was decisively ahead, although there could be changes once absentee ballots were tallied. When I finally walked out into the November drizzle, I ran into Tom and we had a celebratory hug.

"Have you, perhaps, ever thought about leaving the campaign trail and its 16-hour-days, for a job at City Hall?" I asked the question tentatively, knowing that—if I were elected—I would need to hire a chief of staff.

"Too early," Tom said brusquely. He didn't charge me a quarter for the "perhaps." But I thought his answer translated as "no way."

The exchange was a bit of a downer. I sighed and slipped behind the wheel of Green Pea, the car's backseat littered with campaign mailers, remittance envelopes, and draft questionnaires. I drove north alone. Once again, I felt light-headed and disoriented.

When I reached home, I pulled into the driveway in front of my boarded-up garage. My headlights illuminated the boards that Larry Cobb's workmen had hammered across the damaged garage opening. I turned off the car engine and just sat there looking and laughing until tears ran down both cheeks.

Someone had spray painted a bold message across the particle boards. Premature but welcome, it read: "City Council Parking Only."

Seattle City Light's Ross Dam and Powerhouse, built as part of the Skagit
River Hydroelectric Project. *Seattle Municipal Archives 138172*

13

Let There Be Light, 2004–2008

My first job in January 2004 as a brand new, very green Seattle city councilmember was to confirm a new City Light superintendent, the highest paid position in city government.

The former superintendent, Gary Zarker, had resigned in June 2003 realizing he lacked council support for reconfirmation. His resignation came after stormy public hearings and a study showing widespread employee dissatisfaction. Zarker's troubles stemmed partly from the Enron crisis that led to a staggering 58 percent boost in city electric rates.

As one of three new councilmembers, I had little say when it came to picking a committee chairmanship (each councilmember has one). I had thought that Energy and Environment, the committee overseeing City Light, would likely go to newly elected councilmember David Della. He had successfully campaigned against Heidi Wills, the former Energy Committee chair, smearing her on billboards as "Rate-Hike Heidi." But I had guessed wrong. Della preferred chairing Parks and Recreation.

In mid-December, even before the January swearing-in ceremonies, I was invited for happy hour drinks at Il Terrazzo Carmine, a Pioneer Square restaurant. There I was pressured by Council President Jan Drago and Councilmembers Richard Conlin and Jim Compton to take over the Energy Committee, the one no one else wanted. I gulped and accepted with a shudder.

I knew City Light, the city-owned electric utility, was heavily in debt. To keep energy prices affordable during the 2002 Enron financial scandal, City Light had borrowed $600 million to buy power. The utility owed an amount equal to 90 percent of its assessed valuation. Once considered the city's most priceless asset, the municipal utility was nearly broke and essentially leaderless, operating with an interim superintendent.

On the positive side, the only way City Light could go was up. So with a steep learning curve ahead, I took the opportunity to talk to the mayor's staff about their search for a new superintendent.

It is true that I owed a great deal to Mayor Greg Nickels. Almost from the beginning, he had endorsed my election campaign, not being a fan of Judy Nicastro, the incumbent. She had regularly thwarted his plans, had worked to slash his office budget, and even threatened to run for mayor against him. A political newbie, I was deeply grateful for Nickels' support, unusual since most mayors played safe, either endorsing incumbents or staying neutral.

My office was not fully staffed that January, but my former campaign manager, Tom Van Bronkhorst, had agreed to sign on as chief of staff, and a friend, Dawn Todd, had waded in to take over scheduling duties. Minutes after moving into our City Hall offices (furniture not even arranged), Dawn took a call from Deputy Mayor Tim Ceis (pronounced "cease") requesting an early meeting. She may have offended him by innocently asking how to spell his name.

Most of us who followed city politics already knew how to spell "Ceis," a former chief of staff to King County Executive Ron Sims. A power player who allegedly took no prisoners, Ceis was sometimes called "a kneecapper" or "a hatchet man." But he was best known, not entirely affectionately, as "the Shark."

Ceis arrived for our meeting along with Michael Mann, the mayor's council liaison, and Bob Royer, head of communications at City Light. They said that Mayor Nickels planned to appoint Jorge Carrasco as the new City Light superintendent. Carrasco, former head of a Bay Area water utility, was the top pick of three candidates recommended by a citizens' advisory committee.

They filled me in on Carrasco's background. He had been a city manager in Austin, Texas, and Scottsdale, Arizona, and had headed utilities in New Jersey and the East Bay Area in California. He had built a solid career as a manager, but admittedly was not up to date on electrical energy issues.

Ceis wanted to know: "How soon can your committee confirm him?" Hardly knowing what I was doing, I said we'd try to get confirmation within a month's time.

Little did I know that, in view of City Light's history, I was being wildly optimistic. During former Mayor Charles Royer's tenure, the Council had held 13 public hearings and had debated for four months before confirming one City Light superintendent by a narrow 5–4 vote. The job of confirming a candidate to head City Light was not for the faint of heart.

Unaware of how to do a confirmation, my aide Tom and I set out to find out all we could about Carrasco's background. We went about it as we had in our former roles: me as if I were doing investigative reporting for a newspaper; Tom as if he were conducting research on an opposition candidate. We had support from council central staffers Bill Alves and Carol Butler. But, for the two of us, it was virgin territory.

Our first decision was to hire a clipping service to collect articles from cities where Carrasco had once worked. We arranged for two public hearings at City Hall, one daytime and the other a town hall meeting in the evening. The aim was to hear from as many voices as possible.

Meanwhile, I got on the phone and started calling mayors, councilmembers, and city employees, researching Carrasco's career. The response was mixed. From a former mayor of Scottsdale, I heard that he had been one of their best city managers ever. But from a utility consultant in California I heard that he was a volatile boss, that he sometimes yelled at employees, and that he was the last person we should hire. The consultant ended our phone conversation saying, "Hire him and you'll be sorry."

When I contacted past and present Austin councilmembers, I heard Carrasco's management style lauded by some, but criticized by others as "unyielding" and "aloof." As Austin's city manager, he had laid off dozens of workers without notifying the council and had kept councilmembers in the dark about budgets. He also had replaced building inspectors with private contract workers. It soon became apparent that, as a manager, Carrasco had been effective but polarizing.

My staff processed hundreds of pages of press clippings, bound into phone-book-sized binders, shared first with Energy Committee members David Della and Nick Licata, and then with others on the council. The clippings were also made available in the city clerk's office for anyone to read.

The stories ranged from straightforward political reportage to an entertaining feature story that told how Carrasco had come to the rescue of his next-door neighbor in Austin. The neighbor called him when she discovered a skunk in her kitchen. After the local fire department's initial failure at skunk removal, Carrasco succeeded in luring the pesky beast outside.

Stirring up matters locally, the *Stranger*, an alternative paper known for its "gotcha" approach, pointed out that Seattle's official city website had prematurely listed Carrasco as "City Light Superintendent." Since he had not yet been confirmed, it would have been more accurate to identify him as "a candidate for superintendent." The website was quickly corrected.

The January 20 town hall hearing on Carrasco's confirmation was memorable for its contrasting opinions. We heard from the mayor's office strongly supporting the nominee. Deputy Mayor Ceis dubbed him "the perfect candidate."

We also heard from dozens of City Light employees who showed up to protest Carrasco's lack of experience with electric utilities. Union members sounded the alarm over his background leading New Jersey's American Water Works, a utility that had specialized in buying up other utilities. Some of those testifying warned that, once confirmed, he would outsource city services and try to privatize City Light.

How strong was Carrasco's allegiance to municipal power? At the hearing, he voiced his staunch support for keeping City Light public, but he did waiver when it came to the subject of outsourcing. He characterized it as a way "to be more operationally efficient." That was not what the dozens of City Light workers at the public hearing wanted to hear.

When my committee met the following Tuesday, David Della and I, convinced that City Light needed a strong manager, voted to recommend approval of Carrasco. The other committee member, veteran councilmember Nick Licata, had reservations. He withheld approval and moved to postpone a full council vote.

The delay was disappointing after weeks of vetting Carrasco's nomination. But it was a valuable lesson. I discovered how important it is to count votes. It didn't matter how well-crafted or researched a proposal; what mattered was how many councilmembers would vote "yes." I belatedly remembered the words of Sam Smith, a former council president, who famously said, "Five votes is policy."

Sam Smith's five-vote maxim was among the many lessons that we would learn during the busy month of January 2004. Because the 2003 election had produced three new councilmembers, highest council turnover in 35 years, Council President Jan Drago had arranged a month-long series of briefings. It gave new councilmembers and their staffers an opportunity to learn how City Hall functioned.

From the city clerk, we had instruction in parliamentary procedure as used by the city council. What did it mean to "call for the previous question" or to "table a motion?" If Robert's Rules of Order were not previously part of our lives, they would be now. We learned, too, that we must always allot time for public comment at each of our committee meetings, as well as before full council meetings.

Also looming were the many PDRs: Public Disclosure Requests. As the result of a specific request, we would have to produce promptly any letter or email we received on that subject, any letter or memo that we might have written. Nothing would remain confidential. Nor could more than four councilmembers meet behind closed doors. Such meetings violate the law and would be subject to stiff fines. Public business had to be conducted in public.

"You will be sued while you are in office," City Attorney Tom Carr assured us. The good news, he said, was that the city's law department would defend us, provided we were acting within our scope as councilmembers.

We were warned that we dare not open our own mail or emails. That was the job for a staff member who would screen the mail first, lest we accidentally read about a land use decision—known as a "quasi-judicial decision"—prior to that issue coming before the council. Any councilmember who slipped up would have to recuse him or herself and skip a vote on that particular issue.

While undergoing Council 101 training, my staff and I continued working every spare moment on the Carrasco appointment. The definitive vote was rescheduled to come before the full nine-member city council February 2. This time, I knew to reach out to other councilmembers, making sure they had all the materials and information they needed to make a decision. I was carefully counting votes.

My crash course in the confirmation process culminated in approval of Carrasco by the full council. The vote was unanimous; even Licata said "yes." Councilmember Jim Compton took the opportunity to point out that Carrasco had signed and agreed to a performance contract listing goals and expectations and would receive a $210,000 city salary, tops in the city. Other councilmembers expressed approval if not outright enthusiasm. Council president Jan Drago told Carrasco he was "the right person for the job."

It had taken almost exactly one month to confirm the new superintendent. And, with a City Light leader in place, my staff (aug-

Superintendent Jorge Carrasco and the new committee chair touring a City Light substation, September 2006. *Seattle Municipal Archives, Item 170600*

mented by the addition of Jeannine Souki) would continue wrestling with critical City Light issues for the next four years. Oversight meant constant pressure from large energy consumers such as the Boeing Company and Nuccor Steel. The big guns were first in line, lobbying for lower electric rates.

Oversight also meant hearing from City Light's Citizen's Advisory Committee, a panel of energy-savvy citizens who devoted time to advising the council. In one of its annual reports, the citizens—fiscally wise but politically naïve—pushed for a change in governance: The report argued that the committee itself should take over full supervision of City Light, cutting out the council entirely. The recommendation, needless to say, was politely received, but dead on arrival.

During my four years as Energy Committee chair, Seattle was able to take credit and even win trophies for City Light's aggressive conservation efforts, preserving habitat, and regulating stream flows to assist salmon spawning.

Supervising the goat squad hired by Seattle City Light to clear blackberries and other invasive plants around utilities. *Seattle Municipal Archives, Item 170599*

Another opportunity for mutual back-patting was the stunning news that City Light would be going carbon neutral in 2005, the first U.S. utility to achieve that status. It helped that the bulk of the city's electrical needs were met by renewable hydro-powered dams. But reaching zero carbon emissions was still an admirable achievement.

During those years, City Light's biggest challenge was the Hanuk-kah Eve windstorm that slammed the city December 14 and 15, 2006. The storm was preceded by a record 16 inches of rainfall in November. When gale-force winds struck, rain-sodden trees and limbs toppled, wiping away power lines. In western Washington, the storm left 1.8 million residences without electricity; 180,000 of those were City Light customers.

In the days after the storm, the weather turned bitter cold, adding to the city's woes. I set to work with the mayor's office to establish shelters for people who had been left in the dark and cold. Our first attempt partly backfired when hundreds were directed to a South Seattle Community Center only to discover that the community center also was without power.

My office crew and I circled the city, visiting shelters staffed with hard-working Park Department employees who had been pressed into service. They provided hot meals and set up cots. In North Seattle, they sent a van to nearby retirement homes and escorted elderly residents, some stranded in cold, dark rooms, to warmth at the Bitter Lake Community Center. There were many unsung heroes and heart-warming stories in the aftermath of the storm.

City Light line workers labored day and night, putting in 17-hour shifts. They had to virtually rebuild the city's electrical distribution system. Because other utilities in the region had been similarly impacted by the storm, nearby reinforcements were unavailable. Eventually City Light would seek help from utilities as far away as the Midwest.

Meanwhile, my office fielded hundreds of calls from customers unable to report outages directly to City Light's overloaded phone lines. Even when they reached the call center, customers often came away aggrieved, unable to get any idea when power would be restored.

Many called my office. Some merely wanted the latest information, others were outraged, demanding—somewhat futilely—that we restore their power immediately. Several said: "Right now or else." We truly felt everyone's anguish as it was only days until the Christmas holiday. City Light customers were facing one of the bleakest pre-holiday seasons in memory.

We heard sad stories about cancelled holiday events and ceremonies, about disabled customers who, without electricity to power elevators, were trapped in dark, heatless, multi-story buildings. And we heard from residents who for various reasons couldn't remain in their homes. Some were forced to seek increasingly scarce space in city hotels.

Before power was fully restored, 13 people in the region died, most by carbon monoxide poisoning due to unsafe use of barbecues and generators. Seattle actress Kate Fleming drowned in her flooded basement on the evening of December 14. Others died when crushed by falling trees. A man and his dog were electrocuted by a downed power line.

Local hospitals treated several hundred victims of carbon monoxide poisoning. Most were newly-arrived immigrants. The carbon monoxide deaths and injuries prompted the *Seattle Times* to devote its entire December 20 front page to warnings that explained the danger of indoor charcoal use, translated into six languages.

As part of my due diligence, I visited the City Light call center and talked to the valiant employees who were doing their utmost to dispense what little information they could supply. Some call center workers, their own homes without power, were barely given time off to dash home for a change of clothing.

There was some encouraging news: Almost 50 percent of city outages were restored within the first 48 hours. But that meant that tens of thousands still remained in the dark and would be without power for days to come. Main distribution lines, torn down by the storm, first had to be reconstructed before feeder lines could be powered. I spent hours on the phone with Superintendent Carrasco getting daily updates and with Tim Ceis checking on shelters and services.

Ceis astutely summed up the dismal situation saying, "If we don't get power back by Christmas, we all may as well quit."

During the height of the emergency, I received two death threats, one of them serious enough for referral to the Seattle Police Department. The angry male caller had said that, with the naked eye, he could see a broken wire dangling from a nearby pole. He added that we needed only to reconnect that wire and his electricity would be back on. Then he delivered his ultimatum: "Restore my power. Or I will kill you."

Given the level of anger and frustration, I was grateful when I could finally breathe with relief and answer phone calls without dread. Power throughout the city was fully restored two days before Christmas. The utility had played no favorites. Among the last to see light was the Leschi home of Councilmember Conlin, eight days and 17 hours without power.

Even before all the lights were back on, we as councilmembers began asking questions about the storm response. How widespread was the power outage? What were the contributing factors? How could we do better in future incidents?

Superintendent Carrasco provided the council with a preliminary after-action report. He enlisted a review panel of utility executives from across the country and Canada. He also hired Davis Consulting to prepare a comprehensive storm report.

The 100-page Davis report, delivered in May 2007, was fascinating to those of us who lived through the challenging time. It provided a timeline, detailed what worked and what didn't. The report concluded with recommendations for future actions. Among items on the lengthy to-do list: faster post-storm damage assessment, improved communications, mutual assistance pacts with out-of-area utilities, and more frequent tree trimming.

Customer service also needed improvement. The report called for better technology and recommended training other City Light employees as backup to assist the call center during an emergency. The report said customers "should be able to report outages, hear a sense of urgency and receive better estimates on when power would be restored."

Given the magnitude of damage, the Davis report gave City Light generally good marks for the length of time it took to restore power throughout the system. When it came to the report's recommendations, steps were already underway to improve the utility's response and restoration skills.

By the end of my four years as chair of the Energy and Environment committee, the utility was in a better place. It was on track to reduce its debt from nearly 90 percent to 65 percent. City Light also began the important but lengthy process of relicensing Boundary Dam, the utility's largest power source.

Finally, with all this forward progress, the council was able to consider lowering electric rates—for the first time ever. My committee and then full council voted an 8.4 percent across the board reduction. The unprecedented rate decrease made up for the steep hikes imposed during the Enron debacle. As a result, Seattle was offering the lowest and most stable electrical rates of any U.S. city, no small achievement.

Looking back on Carrasco's leadership over the period he served—11 years in all—one could feel reasonably good about that initial 2004 confirmation.

During his tenure, Carrasco worked with four Energy Committee chairs and served under a parade of mayors, three in all. He had done well with Mayor Nickels who had initially hired him. When Mayor Mike McGinn took over the seventh-floor executive offices, he axed many of the Nickels people. One notable exception to the exodus was Carrasco. The City Light superintendent allegedly dared McGinn to go ahead and fire him. He told McGinn to see what talent he could find to head a billion-dollar operation relying on the comparatively modest salary he had been receiving.

McGinn, who was focused narrowly on environmental and transportation issues, appeared content to leave Carrasco in place rather than devote muscle and resources to replacing him.

The same was true when Mayor Ed Murray took over. Murray had far more pressing issues at the beginning of his term in office. A minimum wage proposal, complex policing issues, and the push for increased density took precedence over changes at City Light. At first it was a matter of "if it ain't broke, don't fix it," but then a series of untoward events took over. And, unfortunately, the final months of Carrasco's lengthy tenure turned sour, marred by embarrassing pratfalls.

In his final years, Carrasco was duped by a pair of con-men—"Chief Little Bear" and "Joe Wolf"—posing as Native Americans. They arrived at City Light's offices clad in full Native American regalia. The scammers persuaded Carrasco to donate scrap copper wire supposedly to an art project for disabled Cherokee children. King County prosecutors later discovered the con-men were not Native Americans, the art project was non-existent, and the two men had been working a similar scheme on others in the Puget Sound region and across the country.

Rather than a small donation of scrap wire, the scammers made off with 21 tons of wire, valued at $120,000. It was surprising that Carrasco, a hard-driving executive, would fall for such a sleazy plot.

Equally embarrassing was discovery that the superintendent—now titled "general manager"—had hired Brand.com to scrub and reorder his internet profile so that background searches would prioritize positive reports.

Then there was the matter of an abortive salary increase. Although Carrasco had received modest pay increases over the years, his salary of $249,348 a year was far below the compensation given top electric utility managers, even managers of public utilities.

Carrasco had privately asked the mayor for a pay increase of up to $120,000. After the mayor agreed to a $60,000 raise, Carrasco at first denied to media that the pay raise had been his idea, leaving the embarrassed mayor with little choice but to rescind the pay request.

Carrasco issued a belated public apology over his missteps, but it finally was time to consider stepping down. He resigned in May 2015, taking an opportunity to underscore some of his achievements. His accomplishments were considerable: fiscal stabilization of a once teetering utility, an improved work safety record, better customer service, and City Light's leadership on conservation. Carrasco helped preserve the utility's reputation as the nation's cleanest, most affordable source of electric power.

There may have been cold feet in the beginning. But, in the end, the results he had achieved were no small achievement.

14

Be Careful What
You Wish For, 2008–2012

M y Swedish grandmother had rules to live by. Her maxims were
corny but they mostly steered us in the right direction. One of
her favorites: Be careful what you wish for; you just might get it.

It was 2008 and I had just been comfortably reelected to a second
term on the Seattle City Council. I had fought and won a battle with
Councilmember Nick Licata over who would chair the council's most
important committee: Finance and Budget.

Having learned to count votes during my first four-year term,
I lobbied my colleagues hard and managed to tally five solid votes.
Council President Richard Conlin, who had remained neutral, con-
ceded: "Guess you're the winner."

Had I known what lay ahead (the economy was about to tank),
I might have cast my vote for Nick. At the very least, I would have
resorted to gallows humor. As comedian Steve Martin once said: "First
the doctor told me the good news: I was going to have a disease named
after me."

My own good news was they didn't name the worst recession since
the Great Depression after me; but that didn't make the job any less
painful. Be very careful what you wish for.

Seattle, like other Washington cities, has finite resources. When
bad times hit, when development slows and business and sales taxes
slump, the city collects less tax revenue. Recession lands a double
whammy. When times are bad, needs are greatest.

The recession struck Seattle, as downturns often do, after the
slump hit major areas of the nation. But, when the recession slammed
Seattle, it struck sharp and hard and it stayed around longer. One of
the most significant casualties was Seattle-based Washington Mutual,
the nation's largest savings and loan bank, the one we called "WaMu."

WaMu had become hopelessly entangled in the nation-wide housing bubble. Lax lending standards and subprime mortgages helped push the bank to the brink. Federal regulators forced WaMu into receivership in September 2008. The feds took over and then sold the bank at fire-sale prices to JPMorgan Chase. Jamie Dimon, Chase CEO, had long been salivating over the prospect of acquiring the outfit that advertised itself as "The Friend of the Family."

The WaMu debacle will go down in history books as the largest bank failure in the nation's history. Founded right after the 1889 Great Seattle Fire, the bank had prospered for over 100 years, weathering the region's ups and downs until caught up in the housing disaster known as "the Big Short."

Just days following the bank's ignominious failure, Mayor Greg Nickels delivered his proposed 2009–10 budget to the Seattle City Council. It was a cautious budget, totaling slightly less than the previous year's outlay. For the most part, the mayor and Dwight Dively, his veteran budget director, had respected the council's written request to fully fund public safety and human services. In Seattle, the mayor first proposes the budget, but then the council spends eight weeks questioning, examining, and refining—making sausage—before voting on a final version.

During those weeks, councilmembers advocated individually for their pet projects, but there was little wiggle room. With help from Ben Noble, the legislative department's budget analyst, I had insisted that, if a councilmember wanted to add an item to the budget, he or she had to find an equivalent cut. Unlike federal and state governments, the city has to pass a balanced budget and cannot spend money it doesn't have.

Councilmembers weren't the only ones advocating for budget changes and additions. Hundreds of residents also wanted to weigh in. We scheduled public hearings in different areas across the city, as well as a formal public hearing in the city council chambers.

We were seeking advice from people about their priorities. The main questions: What do we do in tough times? What are the city's core services? And what can a city do for you that you cannot get elsewhere?

On one weekday evening an estimated 500 citizens, standing room only, packed into the New Holly Gathering Hall in southeast Seattle to tell councilmembers what mattered most to them. More than 85 of those attending signed up to speak for two minutes and speak they did.

They shared their passion for parks. They voiced concern for social services, for food banks, shelters, and meals programs, and they deplored the possible loss of the library's beloved Bookmobile. The most passionate concerns were for parks and libraries. That is where the city touches the largest, most diverse group of people. Who might be affected if those library services were curtailed? One gentleman put it simply, "Only just Seattleites from seven years to 80."

That hearing featured humor and pathos, cute kids and hand-made drawings. Fathers spoke with pride about their children who trained in "Rowing for Kids" programs and who later went on to earn college scholarships. Moms pleaded to continue Seattle Parks' specialized programs for the developmentally disabled. Gray-haired residents wanted more classes and services at senior centers.

One Queen Anne resident came to the microphone shepherding five adorable youngsters, dressed in brightly colored swimsuits. She said she had planned to ask the city to please, please not limit hours at their neighborhood swimming pool.

But she concluded: "After being here and listening for over an hour, I also support homeless shelters. Please put shelters ahead of the pool."

Generosity of spirit was a common theme at that hearing. The audience warmly applauded speakers who spoke for causes other than their own. It was an uplifting evening; but for those of us faced with the feeble state of the city's treasury, it was a heart-breaking exercise. How do you rank important services when there is simply not enough money?

That public hearing and others like it would be repeated more than a dozen times during my years as Finance and Budget Chair. It was the leanest four years in anyone's recent memory, often compared to the Great Depression of the 1930s.

Not only were there four anemic annual budgets to consider, but during the recession there also were midterm budget reductions. As city revenues dwindled, the budget had to be trimmed back, departments and services continually downsized. It was essential for councilmembers to have a hand in those critical decisions.

How to accomplish that? It was decided that, since we could not hold closed-door meetings with a quorum (five) present, there would be four-member briefings on the mayor's proposed cuts. Those four in turn would brief other councilmembers.

A bit of comic relief occurred that first lean year when *Seattle Times* reporter Emily Heffter tried to follow councilmembers into a midyear budget briefing. When the councilmembers filed past, Emily was sitting in an outer office talking to Tom Van Bronkhorst, my chief of staff. Emily, a tall, athletic woman, rose to follow us, but Tom reached up, grabbed her shoulder strap, held her back, and shook his head.

Tom explained that the briefings were for information only, that no decisions were being made, no votes taken, and therefore they were not open to media. The shoulder strap incident made news as a "gotcha" story in the *Seattle Times* that made it seem as if Tom had manhandled a reporter and violated press freedom. There is some meager humor even in the glummest times.

Budget reductions—10 percent in 2009 and more later—were concentrated in the city's larger departments with the exception of public safety and the human services that councilmembers determined to keep intact. That meant all other departments (especially large ones like transportation and parks) would have to be slashed 15 percent or more.

It was a dismal exercise. If there was any saving grace, it was that Mayor Nickels and the Budget Director Dively worked to keep the council fully briefed and engaged.

In tough times, we were forced to get creative. One budget was rescued in the final week when Councilmember Conlin discovered we could bank a few million by raising the utility tax on water. Another budget was saved by a percentage increase in internet taxes.

While working to balance the budget with drastically reduced revenue, there were few things we did not consider. We boosted user fees and raised parking fines. We charged more to use Park Department fields, more to swim in a city pool. We slashed consulting fees, axed office supplies and non-mandatory training.

We insisted that non-essential city travel be eliminated. We discovered we could raise the commercial parking tax from 10 percent to 12.5 percent. We even went to the voters for help and they approved a .02 percent sales tax increase. In the countdown to the Thanksgiving budget-passing deadline, I felt like more of a skinflint than Dickens' Ebenezer Scrooge, more parsimonious than Eliot's Silas Marner.

There were layoffs, several hundred of them. In the first two years of the recession, Deputy Mayor Tim Ceis worked with city's unions and negotiated concessions. Unionized city workers accepted unpaid furloughs rather than face even larger layoffs. Without being asked, city librarians and other library workers voluntarily agreed to take unpaid furloughs. They did so throughout the recession years.

Although it was mostly symbolic, I too took "unpaid furlough." Since my salary could not be altered—raised or lowered—during my term of office, I voluntarily donated back to the city two weeks' pay. When I discovered I could specify where the money would go, I wrote separate checks to the city's Animal Shelter, to veterinary care for injured strays, and to Bridge, the city's program to rescue prostituted teens.

Although I urged other councilmembers to do the same, I was joined only by Tim Burgess and Sally Clark. One councilmember sent an angry email protesting that his salary was his own business. He did not appreciate colleagues asking him to forego a portion of his wages. Contributing two week's pay was more symbolic than helpful when you're struggling with a multi-billion-dollar budget, but the thought did matter.

Wobbly as it was, the city's multi-year budget balancing act was further upset when Mayor Nickels failed in his reelection bid. He had been damaged by failure to clear the streets promptly during a December 2008 snow storm. He came in third in the August 2009 primary election.

The general election race became a battle between the two top mayoral contenders: Joe Mallahan, a T-Mobile executive, and Mike McGinn, a lawyer and former state Sierra Club president.

In November, McGinn emerged on top, squeaking through with 51.4 percent of the vote. His platform had focused on increasing city support for the schools, enhancing broadband access, and improving transportation, especially for pedestrians and bicyclists.

Throughout the mayoral campaign, McGinn had vigorously opposed the state's plan to construct a deep-bore waterfront tunnel. McGinn argued that the Alaskan Way Viaduct should simply be torn down and traffic—100,000 vehicles per day—routed to crowded surface streets and the heavily-travelled I-5 freeway.

Days prior to his November 2009 election, McGinn did an about-face, reassuring citizens that, if elected, he would honor the city's previous commitments to the deep-bore tunnel. It was an empty, eleventh-hour promise, one he would later find ways to sabotage.

McGinn had his own ideas on city budget priorities. At his swearing-in speech in January 2010 he initially vowed to fire 200 of the city's strategic advisers. His scorched-earth policies, the missteps of a newbie, did not endear him at City Hall. Nor did his decision to fill the mayor's office with a crew of young campaign staffers who lacked government experience.

One of McGinn's early decisions was to replace veteran Budget Director Dwight Dively with Beth Goldberg, a former deputy finance

Mayor McGinn delivers his 2011 budget speech at Rainier Beach Community Center, September 2010. *Seattle Municipal Archives, Item 165196*

director at King County. Within days, Dively, who had managed the city's budget office for 16 years, was scooped up by King County Executive Dow Constantine to take over the county's Office of Management and Budget.

This was worrisome news for the city council. We had worked well with Dively, a fiscal wizard who in addition to his city position taught classes on municipal finance at the University of Washington's Evans School. Before Dively left, we met for an exit interview. Dively said the city should make every effort to earn and maintain high bond ratings, thus saving millions on debt financing. He also stressed the need to keep the recession-impacted city pension system stable and well-funded.

Besides firing Dively, McGinn was finding other ways to irritate the Seattle City Council and impact city finances. Just 15 days after taking over as mayor, he scheduled a last-minute press conference on the waterfront. He arrived on bicycle and announced his plans for a $241-million levy to replace the city's deteriorating seawall. He said he planned to hold a special election in the spring to decide the issue.

As councilmembers, we were blindsided. That morning, we were meeting offsite for our annual day-long retreat. We first learned of the new mayor's plans around noon. Cell phones rang and we began receiving reporters' calls asking for our reactions to McGinn's sudden bombshell.

Councilmembers later learned that, when speaking at the press conference, McGinn told the media that, no, his seawall levy proposal wasn't prompted by his earlier opposition to the deep-bore tunnel. He insisted it was merely out of concern for public safety. After all, he said, "Suppose the seawall were to collapse?"

McGinn brandished a survey, conducted by Bill Broadhead, his own campaign consultant, and paid for by $800 out of McGinn's own pocket. The survey indicated that 70 percent of likely voters favored a seawall levy.

Back from the retreat, a skeptical city council drafted a letter to the mayor requesting a more orderly process. First there needed to be a complete analysis and reliable cost estimates. Eight councilmembers signed the letter; only Mike O'Brien, a biking buddy of the mayor's, opted not to sign.

McGinn's next move was to create a new position in his office. The mayor hired David Hiller, advocacy director at Cascade Bicycle Club as his transportation adviser—some said "bike czar"—with a $95,000 salary. Hiller went to work on the mayor's agenda, promoting "road diets" (turning four-lane arterials into three lane streets with separate bicycle lanes) and bike trails, and opposing construction of the deep-bore tunnel as well as state plans to replace the deteriorating SR 520 floating bridge.

Two years into McGinn's term, the council voted 8–1 to give the state approval on the tunnel right-of-way. Only O'Brien voted "no." McGinn, in turn, vetoed the ordinance. When the council voted to override the veto, McGinn and O'Brien worked with tunnel foes to gather signatures on an anti-tunnel referendum. Although Proposition 1 was only an advisory vote, tunnel opponents believed the referendum would give citizens an opportunity to weigh in and express themselves.

Two of McGinn's staff took a leave of absence to run the anti-tunnel "Protect Seattle Now" campaign, while Dan Nolte of Councilmember Sally Clark's office left to take over the pro-tunnel campaign, "Let's Move Forward."

Meanwhile at City Hall, the council was still dealing with the budget squeeze and with McGinn's differing priorities. His budget proposed hundreds of lay-offs, reduced parks maintenance, put off street repairs, limited community center hours, and cut into police and library services. The council had authorized increases to the police force—105 more police in five years—but the department under McGinn failed to hire additional cops.

On August 16, 2011, the vote on Proposition 1, the referendum on the deep-bore tunnel, resulted in a 60 percent favorable ("yes" to the tunnel) vote. It was a full 10 years since the Alaskan Way Viaduct had been weakened by the 2001 Nisqually earthquake. After a decade of discussion, the public was ready to move forward.

McGinn deserved plaudits for at least one prudent budget move. In the summer of 2011, he proposed an ordinance to replenish the city's nearly depleted Rainy Day Fund. The ordinance specified depositing a percentage of new tax receipts (1.9 percent in 2012) into the fund, technically called the Revenue Stabilization Account.

That doesn't sound like revolutionary action, but it was a commendable, fiscally-sound idea. Although the recession was still raging, it was the right time to start rebuilding resources, setting aside funds to cushion future emergencies.

The Rainy Day proposal presented to the council by budget director Beth Goldberg and central staff analyst Ben Noble was thoroughly discussed in the budget committee. At first, the council balked, rejecting action and postponing a decision until after the mayor presented his 2012 budget. The majority reasoned that, if even a modest amount of tax receipts were locked away, there might not be sufficient funds for essential services.

It was hard to overstate the dire state of the city's finances at that point. The city general fund had lost around $107 million in three years. Reserves had all but disappeared. The Parks and Recreation Department had lost nearly a third of its pre-recession funding. And adding insult to injury, the city ended up on Moody's "negative watch" list. If bond-rating agencies further downgraded the city, it would be far more expensive to borrow for such essentials as water mains and electrical distribution.

Painful as it was, replenishing the Rainy Day Fund was essential to the city's future health. Once again, I lobbied my fellow council members for their votes and eventually was able to get 8–0 approval on the plan. Bitter pill or not, the move eventually brought the city's bond rating up to Triple-A levels.

While some of McGinn's fiscal moves were commendable, his handling of the police department was less than admirable. On June 25, 2010, McGinn appointed John Diaz, a thoughtful, soft-spoken officer who had been serving as interim chief of police, to fill the position permanently. Appointing a police chief is arguably the mayor's most important role. But McGinn may have botched the job by making an in-house choice. Although experienced and well-liked by the force, Diaz seemed ill-equipped to make the needed changes.

Police use of force, discriminatory policing, and botching demonstrations like a destructive May Day riot had been an issue in the city for some time. Then in August 2010, Seattle police officer Ian Birk shot and killed John T. Williams, a deaf Native American woodcarver.

The killing was found an "unjustified" use of deadly force. Birk, who was never prosecuted, subsequently resigned. That incident, along with other racially charged police issues, prompted the ACLU and 34 community groups to demand a federal investigation of the Seattle Police Department.

In March 2011, the Department of Justice (DOJ) and the U.S. Attorney's Office, Western Division, launched the investigation. In December the DOJ and attorney's office issued its findings: The Seattle Police Department was engaged in "a pattern or practice of excessive force that violates the U.S. Constitution and federal laws as well as a concern that some of SPD's policies, particularly those related to pedestrian enforcement, could result in discriminatory policing."

Mayor McGinn and Chief Diaz were thunderstruck. Shortly afterwards, they made a rare joint visit to the second-floor council offices to explain the DOJ findings. On a gloomy day shortly before Christmas, they arrived in my office and sat glumly on the blue sofa inherited from my predecessor.

McGinn appeared shaken, Chief Diaz almost bereaved. McGinn stated that meeting the DOJ conditions would cost the city up to $41 million a year—an outsized estimate hastily prepared by the police department. He feared a proposed federal monitor would "become a shadow mayor."

McGinn's response to the DOJ findings was to call a March 28, 2012, press conference and unveil "SPD 20/20: A Vision for the Future." Appearing with Chief Diaz and Assistant Chief Mike Sanford, he told media that Seattle police would reform the department with 20 actions in 20 months. A website with weekly bulletins on SPD progress would be available to the public.

"There's an opportunity in here," McGinn declared. "We're looking to seize that."

The mayor had regained his equilibrium. He put the best face on the response, a collection of worthy promises but few specifics, saying, "Don't let a good crisis go to waste."

After weeks of meetings with DOJ's Civil Rights Division chief Thomas Perez, U.S. Attorney Jenny Durkan, and City Attorney Pete

Holmes, the stubborn mayor was reluctantly persuaded to sign a consent decree with the Department of Justice. One of the features of the July 2012 agreement was the appointment of a Citizens Police Commission to observe the reforms. Formation of the CPC was a definite step forward, one for which McGinn claimed and might actually deserve some credit.

McGinn's four-year term at the city was the most contentious of my 12 years at the city, partly due to the faltering economy, but also because of McGinn's desultory approach to city priorities. The mayor seemed preoccupied with transportation—not with fixing roads, but with road diets. From the beginning of his term, he had adopted an adversarial relationship with the council. It was common to pick up the morning paper and learn for the first time about his latest scheme. Seldom did he provide the courtesy of a briefing to councilmembers.

Nevertheless, I felt incredibly fortunate to chair the Finance and Budget Committee, even when the honor sometimes seemed tarnished by meager resources or by the mayor's divisive behavior. I had the opportunity to steer what scarce resources we had to neighborhood health clinics, to libraries, to domestic violence prevention, to youth programs, and to human services and public safety.

I also used my political capital to co-sponsor, along with Councilmember Nick Licata, a city ordinance that mandated paid sick leave for workers throughout the entire city. Although paid sick leave was progressive legislation, it was unpopular in some business sectors. Restaurateurs who had been my loyal supporters during earlier elections were alienated by my advocacy. I heard from one restaurateur that I should "forget (his) support ever again."

But I took comfort that, after four years heading the Budget and Finance Committee, I was working in a city with a healthy post-recession bond rating, a more stable pension fund and a Rainy Day Fund designed to cushion against future downturns.

Perks of the job: getting to tour the municipal water supply with the hardworking Seattle Public Utilities crew. *Author's collection*

15

Watershed Moves, 2012–2014

The first week of January 2012, I took over a new Seattle City Council committee—Libraries, Utilities, and Seattle Center. Almost immediately, there came a bombshell.

Seattle Public Utilities (SPU) director Ray Hoffman arrived in my office with jolting news: A utility employee had managed to steal more than $1 million dollars. It was the largest embezzlement in Seattle city history and my introduction to oversight of SPU.

Hoffman explained that it had been the job of one Joseph Phan, an SPU project engineer, to meet with customers and estimate the cost of extending or installing water mains. Thought to be a trustworthy employee, Phan had also been collecting deposits and payments for that work. Customers would hand over checks made out to the City of Seattle.

Phan diverted some of those checks to a Bank of America account he opened in 2006. The account was listed in Phan's name and "the city of Sea." Over the next five years, Phan deposited dozens of city checks, banking around $1.1 million. He used the stolen money to pay off his home mortgage and buy houses and other properties.

Once Hoffman and others uncovered the scam, it was referred to the Seattle Police Department and the King County Prosecutor. Phan's scheme had unraveled when a developer called to check on an earlier water-main job, paid for with a check made out to the City of Seattle and handed over to Phan. When asked about the developer's check, the utility staff was mystified. They couldn't find any record of payment.

The theft made for an interesting first few weeks of 2012. My staff and I were kept busy fielding calls from media, hearing from angry ratepayers, briefing other councilmembers, contacting the Seattle city auditor to request a proper audit, and keeping track of steps the utility was taking to tighten financial controls.

To avoid future threats, Hoffman put new procedures and systems into place. He also arranged for the SPU staff to take training in how to spot possible theft. One of the lessons learned: Despite careful precautions, it is almost impossible to safeguard entirely against a clever, determined thief.

Phan, the clever thief, was arrested in March 2012 and charged with 67 counts of first-degree theft and three counts of second-degree theft. Eventually, the city was able to recoup funds from the sale of Phan's properties. Most of the remaining loss was covered through the city's insurance provider.

As Hoffman confided, "The good news is that Joe had a good eye for real estate. The properties he bought increased in value over the years."

Once the Phan case was behind us, working with Seattle Public Utilities could only become better and it did. Hoffman was a dream manager for a city department. He worked tirelessly on the all-important core city services: solid waste, water supply, sewers, and drainage. I appreciated his work and his rapport with staffers, although his casual dress did draw some sidelong glances. Hoffman's imaginative thrift-shop attire, topped with his long, graying pony tail, was an unusual uniform for a top city official.

The committee's grandest moment came when the city council voted, authorizing Seattle Public Utilities to sign a consent decree with the U.S. Department of Justice. The agreement was reached after years of negotiations, years when the city was slapped with and paid large fines for violating the federal Clean Water Act. The historic agreement gave the city time to construct combined sewers, large holding facilities that would prevent storm-related incidents of untreated sewage pouring into local waters. The decree gave Seattle leeway—over a decade—to complete new facilities.

Most importantly, the agreement also allowed the city to make use of green technologies such as rain gardens and rain barrels. These technologies would help prevent raw sewage and toxic overflow from city streets from spilling untreated into Lake Washington and Puget Sound.

On a May morning in 2012, Mayor Mike McGinn and I stood before reporters and television cameras at Gas Works Park, overlooking the waters of Lake Union. We stood at a podium to announce the precedent-setting agreement with a canopy of umbrellas above our heads. As if on cue, the skies opened up to pelting rain.

Although not nearly as globally significant as the consent decree, several smaller successes at SPU were personally rewarding. In particular, I was proudest of an initiative we were calling "No Child Without Water."

From right to left: Seattle Public Utilities director Ray Hoffman; Mayor Mike McGinn; unidentified umbrella-wielding Good Samaritan (possibly a representative of the U.S. Dept. of Justice); and I at a 2012 Sewer Overflow/Stormwater Consent Decree news conference. *Seattle Municipal Archives, Item 183581.*

My aide Carlo Davis and I had been alerted by Doug Edelstein, a Nathan Hale High School teacher, that some of his students were complaining about classmates seated near them. The youngsters smelled bad, having come to school without showering. The reason? Their households' water had been shut off due to unpaid bills.

I soon learned to my sorrow that water shutoffs were not uncommon during the lean recession years. Davis and I, along with aides

Monica Ghosh and Bailey Bauhs, began looking into the situation. We called local charities, churches, and food banks to find out if they were aware of the water-shutoff problems. Had they been asked for help paying delinquent water bills?

What we found out was sobering. Local charities knew many sad stories. They heard about cash-strapped householders who had resorted to borrowing buckets of water from neighbors to wash diapers or flush toilets. Children too often were the victims when parents or caretakers, perhaps choosing instead to cover a mortgage, failed to pay their water bills.

How to fix matters? During a brainstorming session, Susan Sanchez, who oversaw the SPU call center, proposed a solution. She suggested that the problem could be solved by simply expanding low-income emergency assistance—a once-a-year credit—to twice-a-year help for those families with minor children in the home. Given SPU's quarterly billings, that meant there would be no interruption of service.

We held a round table meeting to learn more about water shut-off problems. It was heart-rending to hear the hardship stories told by assistance workers. In only a very few cases had the charities—themselves stretched thin—actually been able to extend help. Among the tales was a personal one, told by a charity worker who, as a youngster, had himself lived in a home without water.

Along with the "No Child Without Water" resolution, we took up and passed proposals to reform low-income rate enrollment, a program that offered reduced rates to qualified low-income customers. Needy seniors had been forced to submit new applications every 18 months. With the committee fix, they needed to do so only every 36 months. As we had learned, low-income seniors seldom grew richer or had more income to report.

And finally we were able to make low-income rates (a discount of 50 percent) available retroactively. Needy customers previously had been forced to wait six months or more before the lower rate kicked in. Reduced rates would now begin on the day the city received a qualified application.

It felt good to be able to work out these fixes, reforms that would cost ratepayers only a few pennies across a region-wide utility system.

No child without water, no long waits for reduced rates, and fewer hassles for the elderly poor.

Meanwhile, the committee members and I continued to work on something we were calling Zero Waste. Seattle had achieved national recognition for its 55.7 percent recycling rate. But we could still do better; San Francisco was claiming 75 percent.

During this time, councilmembers Tom Rasmussen and Richard Conlin and I took a trip to San Francisco to learn from that city's success story. A garbage tour was hardly a glamor junket, but it gave us a chance to see first-hand how San Francisco was managing its solid waste and how restaurants in that city were separating food waste and recyclables from trash.

My companions and I spent one off-duty evening at an upscale Mexican restaurant near San Francisco's Union Square. We ordered drinks and guacamole. After a lengthy wait, we finally received a bowl of seasoned, mashed avocado but no chips. Figuring chips were coming, we waited. Still no chips. A complaint to our waiter finally produced a visit from the chef. The burly, red-faced chef came stomping in.

"You want chips; you better damn well order chips!" he shouted, waving his arms. It was our first and last encounter with an individual we christened the Guacamole Nazi. On the good side, we could report that the restaurant was making efficient use of recycling and composting bins.

Our small delegation also toured a waste recycling plant decorated with imaginative art fashioned from the city's discards. The facility had its own resident artist, a young art student who had won an all-expense-paid, six-month stay at the plant. During his sojourn, he was encouraged to fashion "garbage art" using the endless supply of discarded materials.

We uncovered one of San Francisco's recycling secrets when we toured a city disposal plant on the San Francisco Bay waterfront. On the waterfront? I could scarcely believe the land-poor city could spare a precious waterside site for waste. However, San Francisco had long since shifted marine traffic to the Port of Oakland. What remained was space for a state-of-the art facility that separated waste into reusable components: paper, metals, and plastics. Paper products such as newsprint were compressed into bales and loaded directly onto dockside vessels bound for Asia. The city's efficient waste management operation was not only environmentally sound, but also profitable.

When I returned to Seattle, I was determined to boost our Zero Waste efforts. The first step was passing a law requiring that construction waste be recycled. (Previously it had been treated as garbage.) Then we took the next step in commercial recycling. We drafted a law requiring businesses to separate and recycle glass bottle, and jars, and tin and aluminum cans, just as householders had long been doing.

Commercial recycling was not immediately popular. Businesses and building owners first resisted saying they didn't have space for extra cans and that it would mean hiring additional workers. However, after a few mostly symbolic protests, the business community accepted the new law, which passed the council with ease. To help make it work, particularly for small ma-and-pa eateries, we hired outreach workers to explain how to sort and recycle.

The commercial requirement was guaranteed to quickly bring Seattle's recycling rate to 60 percent. That meant that the city would be spared sending hundreds of rail cars of trash to landfills in Oregon. Sharing top honors with San Francisco, Seattle was a national leader in recycling.

That reputation became even clearer when the National League of Cities met in Seattle in November 2013. Mayors and councilmembers were given a choice of how to spend one afternoon free of meetings. What would officials from other cities want most to see? They had an interesting choice: Meet Bill Gates at Microsoft or meet Jean Godden at Allied Waste, Seattle's main recycling facility. Incredibly, most picked me.

I led the large contingent, several hundred eager local officials, as we toured the mechanized recycling plant south of downtown Seattle. We donned hard hats and navigated through three levels of conveyor belts, fitted with Rube Goldbergian equipment, conveyor belts, air jets, and magnetic arms. Paper and plastic cups were almost magically separated from tin cans and empty drink bottles.

In the aftermath, I fielded dozens of questions. How long would it take for their municipality to assemble a plant like ours? What kind of resistance could you expect from customers? What were the economics? What's the market for selling recycled paper and aluminum?

Never had I dreamed that garbage would be my sweet smell of success.

It was a proud moment in 2015 when Mayor Ed Murray approved paid parental leave for Seattle city employees. *Author's collection.*

16

Wages at War, 2013–2015

Seattle's progressive reputation took a hard hit on "Equal Pay Day," April 8, 2013. That day, the National Partnership for Women and Families (NPWF) published a report revealing that Seattle employers were paying women just 73 cents for every dollar men were earning.

The average gap between men's and women's wages in Seattle was the largest—make that the absolute worst—in the nation. For a working woman, that difference penciled out to more than $16,000 in lost wages every year.

The dismal report was issued on the day of the year women across the United States had to work until in order to catch up to what men earned in the previous year. Nationally, women had to work just over three months longer; in Seattle, women had to work until May.

Seattle's women are not accustomed to being last or worst. On the contrary. The city, along with Washington State, can lay claim to a history of women's firsts.

Washington State granted women the right to vote in 1910, a full decade before passage of the 19th Amendment. That was the second time Washington women had been granted the franchise. Back in 1883 the state's territorial legislature gave the vote to all women citizens—regardless of race or ethnicity. That early privilege, however, was overturned by a state Supreme Court ruling in 1887. (Beer hall owners had sued, fearing women would vote for prohibition; years later they did.)

Seattle was the first major U.S. city to elect a woman mayor, Bertha Knight Landes, in 1926. By 1992, the so-called "Year of the Woman," the Washington State Legislature reached a gender milestone: 40 percent women lawmakers.

At one brief point in 1994, the Seattle City Council could count seven women out of nine councilmembers. The joking question asked on the council dais that year was: "Should we close the men's room?"

The female supermajority of 1994 was not afraid to flex its muscle. When Mayor Norm Rice wanted a new Seattle Central Library constructed beneath a Convention Center annex, the women rebelled. They insisted on a stand-alone central library on the traditional Fourth Avenue site. They called themselves "SLICE," an acronym for Seattle Ladies in Charge of Everything.

Women had long been making their mark in Washington State. What a travesty it was that, at the time of the damning April 2013 report, women were leading in the state. The state then had its second woman governor, Christine Gregoire, and two powerful women senators, Patty Murray and Maria Cantwell.

So the question rankled: Why, with its past record of achievement for women, did the Seattle metropolitan region have the worst gender pay gap in the nation? Was it because of the large number of tech jobs dominated by men? Or perhaps because the region is home to the Boeing Company and the Port of Seattle, employers that pay well and hire mainly men?

Whatever the root causes, it was past time to act. When the jarring news broke, Mayor Mike McGinn was running for reelection. He was quickly put on the defensive by his opponents. No need to wonder why. At the time, the City of Seattle had 10,000 employees; two thirds of those workers were men. Worse still, the city's 25 highest paid officeholders, many of them department heads appointed by McGinn, were men. All of them.

The gender wage gap within city employment stood at 90.5 cents on the dollar. While that was significantly better than the shameful 73-cent gap in the region, wage differences in certain city departments were vast. Male firefighters, for example, averaged $18.60 more per hour than their female associates.

McGinn responded to pointed criticism from his rivals by taking the quick way out. He appointed a task force. He named 15 members, most of them distinguished academics and community leaders. Their task was to recommend ways to narrow the gender imbalance in wages.

At McGinn's urging, I signed on as a member of the Gender Equity in Pay Task Force, co-chaired by YMCA executive Patricia Hayden and Julie Nelson of the city's Office of Civil Rights. At the same time, I urged the mayor to appoint a couple of additional members to represent business and labor. He picked stockbroker Lynn Lindsay and Local 17 union leader Guadalupe Perez.

The task force met for eight months. As one member facetiously pointed out, "nearly enough time to give birth." After interviewing city personnel, hearing many personal stories and considering a range of remedies, the task force agreed to seven general recommendations, each with a series of related actions.

The task force members agreed the wage gap must be addressed, but there was argument over how to proceed. Should there first be a thorough job analysis to determine to what extent female jobs are underpaid? (For instance: should landscape architects—mostly well-educated women—be paid as much as City Light meter readers—mostly men?) Once a proposed job analysis was completed, should there be a strategy to bring pay in line, upping wages where needed? And what about city unions and contractual agreements?

Cost of the extensive job analysis was estimated at $500,000 and adjustment of pay rates to remove bias could run as high as $10 to $12 million. Some thought the up-front costs too large in a city barely recovering from the recession. Others (myself included) believed it would be better to begin first with other recommendations: recruiting women, training women for promotion, providing paid parental leave, and addressing gender equity issues beyond city government.

One stumbling block was that, by the time the task force was readying its final report, Mayor McGinn was no longer mayor. He lost his bid for reelection on November 5, 2013, and had completed his single four-year term.

In January 2014 Ed Murray took over as the city's new mayor, and there were significant changes at City Hall. McGinn had surrounded himself with a largely male, bicycle-riding personal staff; Murray brought in a more diverse and experienced crew, including two women deputy mayors, Kate Joncas and Hyeok Kim. While McGinn often kept the city council in the dark about his latest schemes; Murray prepared to act more collaboratively with councilmembers.

Like many city councilmembers, I had more personal time with Mayor Murray in the first few months of his term than I had with Mayor

McGinn in four years. Murray visited our council offices and spent time talking about city issues. He recalled that during his campaign he had promised to work on gender equity, as he had on human rights in the legislature. Now he was pledging to implement the gender task force findings. As he told me: "How could I not? Otherwise I'd hear from my five sisters."

The task force report offered further insight into why narrowing the wage gap matters. Although we had learned that Seattle's city government had a smaller pay gap—90 cents on the dollar—than the region's 73-cent differential, several city departments (fire, police, City Light, and the law department) showed wide pay disparities. For female employees of color, the city pay gap loomed larger. Asian women were earning 85 cents on the dollar; Latina women, 83 cents; African American women, 79 cents. Race obviously contributed to the wage differential and needed to be addressed.

On March 26, 2014, the task force formally issued its report. By then, I had taken over chairmanship of a new committee: Parks, Libraries, Seattle Center, and Gender Equity. For the first time, gender equity rated a committee. Monitoring and narrowing the wage gap became my committee's responsibility.

The mayor and I agreed that achieving wage equity in the region should start first at City Hall. The council introduced a joint resolution affirming the city's commitment to bringing women's pay and benefits into line with men's. The mayor signed the resolution at a well-attended press conference; his sisters would approve.

We began working on task force recommendations by conducting a department-by-department wage, gender, and racial analysis. Not waiting for the finished analysis, we hired employees to focus on recruiting women for city jobs. We created a permanent program in the city's Office of Civil Rights called the Gender Justice Project, aimed at achieving equal wages for minority employees.

While this work was underway, we were taking additional steps to help working women and families across the city. Councilmember Nick Licata and I co-sponsored legislation requiring Seattle businesses with more than five employees to provide paid sick leave. The ability to take paid time off when ill or when caring for a sick child helps women employees the most.

Equally as important is the $15 minimum wage legislation that Seattle pioneered, first among large U.S. cities. By the time the city's $15 minimum passed in the summer of 2014, there were many backers claiming credit. Part of the glory goes to SEIU 775 union leader David Rolf who actively organized marches and demonstrations, building on an initiative passed in the nearby town of SeaTac.

Some recognition must also go to new Councilmember Kshama Sawant, a Socialist Alternative Party member. She took the stage at many of the organized rallies, bullhorn in hand.

But it was Mayor Murray who deserves the lion's share of credit. Whatever one may think of his later highlighted troubles, Murray was the minimum wage champ. It was he who appointed and worked with the 24-member advisory committee, a diverse group of business, labor, nonprofit, and community leaders. He set them to work in March 2014, arranging for closed-door meetings. He gave them an April 30 deadline.

As the deadline approached, rumors were thicker than discarded coffee cups at City Hall. Conventional wisdom said divisions were so vast the committee would have to disband and agree to disagree. But Murray wasn't about to give up. The mayor told the committee members to keep negotiating.

When matters didn't improve, Murray locked the group into a back room on the seventh floor. He lost his patience and his temper; he erupted, insisting the committee agree to a phased-in plan. There were 21 votes for the final compromise; there were three no votes: Maud Daudon of the Seattle Chamber of Commerce; Craig Dawson of Retail Lockbox, a merchant services company; and Councilmember Sawant, who wanted more immediate action.

The $15 minimum proposal was then sent to the city council to review and revise. The proposal went to a select committee, chaired by Sally Clark. Clark arranged for a series of public forums and hearings, giving councilmembers an opportunity to hear from constituents and business interests. The $15 minimum had strong support as well as vigorous opposition.

During a day-long hearing at Northgate Community Center, we split up into small groups and heard from business men and women, many of them in the restaurant industry. In the small group that I chaired, we listened to restaurateurs and employees who said the $15 minimum was a step too far.

Chef Thierry Rautureau of the restaurant Loulay warned, "We have a very thin bottom line. This may push some of us over the edge."

A server at one of the white-tablecloth restaurants pleaded that, without provision for a tip credit, a $15 minimum wage law wouldn't help her. There were other worries: that employers would hire fewer workers and that their hours would be reduced.

Even though there were understandable concerns about the effect that the $15 minimum would have on city businesses, I personally favored the measure, especially for the lowest paid workers, a large proportion of them women.

After much discussion and with a few modest tweaks, the council voted unanimous approval. Sawant, never reluctant to take full credit, voted affirmatively, but only after she delivered a fiery, finger-pointing speech. She accused her fellow councilmembers of watering down the $15 minimum legislation with provisions such as a tip credit and a smaller training wage. Nevertheless, Seattle would have a $15 minimum wage, the first major U.S. city to do so

With women constituting a lopsided percentage of Seattle's low-paid workers, the city's $15 minimum wage has been critical in the push to narrow the gender wage gap. But other steps also would be needed. Foremost among the task force's recommendations was developing paid parental leave. The United States, incredibly, has stood alone as the only industrialized nation in the world that does not require employers to provide paid parental leave. Nor do most U.S. employers, cities, and states, with only a handful of exceptions.

I first got an earful about the city's lack of paid leave for parents during a chance encounter in a City Hall elevator. Knowing that I was working on gender equity, Marco Lowe, then head of the city's Office of Intergovernmental Relations, used our brief elevator ride for a suggestion. He made it sound like an assignment.

"You need to do something about paid parental leave," Lowe insisted. "This year alone we've had seven babies in our small department. And, with no parental benefit, I've had devil's own time piecing together unused sick leave and vacation time so new parents can have a little time off."

No paid leave to have a newborn or adopt a child? The city had some good benefits, but it had no provision for parental leave. Give birth and you were essentially expected back at work the next day. Parents faced choices: take saved-up sick leave or vacation time or take unpaid leave. Either way there was no assurance your job would be there for you when you returned.

Already I had a sheaf of emails from city workers who had seen their careers and finances upended when they welcomed a newborn. One woman, a city employee, told me she was still in debt three years after the birth of her child. She used up all her sick leave and vacation time and then had taken several extra weeks without pay to care for the new baby. Although still paying the price, she added that, tough as it was, she didn't regret the decision to welcome her son into the world.

Another woman told me how, after childbirth, she had developed serious medical complications that forced her to take unpaid time to recuperate. Then, her child became ill and months passed before she could resume earning a paycheck.

I knew I needed to work on the problem. Thanks to the city council's modest consulting budget I was able to hire a firm to research paid parental leave and find out what was possible. I wanted to know what others municipalities were doing and what it would cost to offer such a benefit.

When the study was completed late in 2014, we found the status quo pretty grim. The study by Towers Watson, a human resources consulting firm, showed that paid parental leaves (PPLs) are still not commonly offered by U.S. employers. Based on a 2014 survey, only 14 percent of U.S. companies allow their employees any paid time off at all.

The situation for cities was equally dismal: no parental leave for Minneapolis, Portland, nor Bellevue; none for Massachusetts or Illinois, none for Group Health, Boeing, Recreational Equipment Inc., nor the University of Washington. The handful that did offer benefits varied: San Francisco gave 12 weeks, but only after that employee used up all discretionary time off; Chicago offered birth mothers six weeks and non-birth parents two weeks.

We reviewed the projected costs and were quickly able to agree on some parameters: the benefit would go to all employees, male and female; the benefit would be available following the birth of a child or upon adoption of a minor child. We decided that the benefit could be used after six months of employment and could be combined with other time off.

It was with some sadness that I discovered that Mayor Murray, perhaps a trifle tone deaf on paid parental leave, had neglected to make provision for a paid parental leave benefit in his proposed 2015 budget.

I refused to let his oversight dampen my resolve. Instead I persuaded my colleagues that it would be wrong to wait another full year before getting started. I talked to each of them, one on one, asking that we add an estimated pot of money to the city budget. I was convinced we could find savings somewhere so paid leaves could start in 2015.

More than just the council had to be won over. First it would be necessary to get approval from the more than two dozen labor unions that represent city workers. I asked David Bracilano, the city's director of labor negotiations, for help. He allowed that, given an extra benefit—something they wouldn't have to bargain over—the unions likely would agree. Nonetheless, union leaders would insist on factoring the provision into contract negotiations.

Because we had no experience with paid parental leave, we were forced to guess at the cost. We looked at the number of dependent children that had been added to city health care plans in 2011 and 2012 and we also factored in the various salary figures we had available.

Given those numbers, the Towers Watson study figured that, in an average year, there would be 230 new parents eligible to take a four-week benefit. The consultants estimated the benefit would cost the city around $1.3 million in the first year.

Fitting an extra $1.3 million into the 2015 budget—a budget still recovering from the long brutal recession—wasn't easy, but councilmembers were convinced it was the right thing to do. Once the city had some experience with the four-week parental benefit, each of us expected the four weeks of paid leave, modest at best, would be increased.

Following passage of the 2015 budget and approval of paid parental leave, the mayor and I had planned to announce the start of PPL for city employees in February. Just days before the announcement, though, there was a glitch. Although we believed labor negotiations had been finalized, there was one exception. The Seattle Public Library, which is governed by a separate board of trustees, had been overlooked. What about paid parental leave for library workers? With help from Patricia Lee, the council's analyst, we worked overnight on negotiations with the library workers union and fortunately were able to reach last minute agreement.

On February 23, 2015, Mayor Murray and I stood at a press conference in the Norman B. Rice Conference Room. Standing under the Chief Seattle seal, we jointly announced the leave benefit, which would become effective in 60 days, mid-May. Seattle became the first municipality in the Northwest to offer the benefit and only one of a handful of cities in the entire nation to do so. Later we would hear from other cities, New York, St. Louis, and Cleveland among them, asking how to provide similar benefits. Our parental benefit became an instant example.

Soon after Seattle passed paid leave, King County announced a 12-week leave, although the county benefit wouldn't kick in until after the employee first exhausted all other time off. Port of Seattle commissioners, too, opted to give workers a four-week paid parental leave, passing legislation in October 13, 2015. Several private employers, including Amazon and Google, announced some generous plans. Parental paid leave, long overdue, was fast becoming the flavor of the day.

U.S. Labor Secretary Thomas Perez, on a cross-country trip, stopped to congratulate Seattle on two important breakthroughs— the $15 minimum wage and paid parental leave. We shared war stories and sampled ice cream at Molly Moon's ice creamery (strawberry for Perez; chocolate for me). With its high minimum wage and paid leave benefits, Molly Moon's had been setting an aggressive worker-friendly example for private employers.

When talking with Secretary Perez, I had to admit that one of the reasons the city of Seattle was able to achieve the benefit is that I had not shut up about it for two full years. Every conversation I had with the mayor, the personnel director, and with my fellow councilmembers turned into a conversation about parental leave.

Joyful as it was to provide the benefit, there was a downside. Parents who had a child just prior to the start of the benefit wouldn't be able to take the leave retroactively. City lawyers insisted on a firm start date. But, even then, I heard from a handful of city employees who said that, although they'd missed out (one by only a couple of weeks), they were happy to work for a city that finally had such a benefit.

The city's paid parental leave benefit, accomplished after two years of effort, took effect May 15, 2015. One of the first to take advantage was mayoral staffer Scott Lindsay. He and his wife, Port Commissioner Courtney Gregoire, welcomed their second daughter in June. By happy coincidence that child is the granddaughter of former Gov. Chris Gregoire.

Our hard work on paid parental leave paid off, better even than we had dreamed. The following year, Seattle was able to increase the paid leave benefit from four to 12 weeks for city workers. Then the Washington Legislature got aboard. After debating the issue for a dozen years, the entire state will soon have both paid sick leave and paid parental leave, benefits financed by a modest tax on employers and employees. The state became only the fifth U.S. state to do so.

Following my committee's giant steps, I had some months left of my third and final term in office. It was an eleventh-hour opportunity to tuck a few more gender equity measures into the 2016 budget. One addition was a pot of money ($1.5 million) to explore an on-site day care center at City Hall. Key to ending the wage gap, finding good child care remains one of the steepest barriers to women fully participating in the workforce. King County's on-site day care in the Chinook Building, heart of the city's government ghetto, serves as a model. The county reserves half of its spaces for county workers, the remainder are drawn from a lengthy waiting list. It's one of the most popular child care centers in downtown Seattle.

As of this writing, plans for a City of Seattle day care facility still remain on hold waiting for the right site. State law requires that centers have adequate outdoor recreational space, something not easily found amidst office towers. But we were able to pass a budget-funded measure ensuring that, whenever new buildings are built, child care needs will be assessed and money set aside for new projects to meet the anticipated need.

We managed a few more gender gains in the 2016 budget. Among them was funding three paid computer-programming internships with the city's internet technology (IT) department. The jobs target women enrolled in accelerated training programs. With thousands of high-tech jobs moving into Seattle, women have remained woefully underemployed in the tech field.

And, finally, Seattle delivered on its promise to expand gender wage equity to the private sector, setting aside $25,000 for regional pay equity initiatives and training. The Greater Seattle Chamber of Commerce's 100% Talent program enlists private employers who promise to take at least three specific steps to end the gender wage gap. So far about a dozen Seattle-based employers have signed on.

The two years that the city's first-ever Gender Equity Committee worked to narrow the wage gap marked a beginning, and represented the best years of my tenure at City Hall. Men and women deserve equal pay for doing equal work. Men and women and workers of color merit equal opportunity. Most of all, men and women need to share equally the rights and responsibilities for holding up the sky. I like to believe we helped with that heavy lifting.

In 2012 Washington became the first state to legalize recreational marijuana. In my last year on the city council, Rebecca Allen, City Council Central Committee staffer (left), my council aide Emily Kim (center), and I had the opportunity to inspect the Seattle Cannabis Co. production facility, January 2015. It was a "heady" experience. *Seattle Municipal Archives, Item 180562*

17

Citizen Godden, 2016

On the first day of January 2016 I completed a third term on the Seattle City Council. I had lost my bid for reelection in the August primary. Although I felt I had more to do and more to contribute, it seemed the right time to hand governing off to others.

My dozen public years had followed 29 years of semi-public life as a reporter, editor, and newspaper columnist.

For the first time in more than 40 years, I was my own private person, answerable only to tax collectors, appliance repairmen, and a garden overgrown with the region's most tenacious and prolific weeds. I was free to think about where I had gone and where I might be heading: Off to a new career? To a rocking chair and the stacks of book I'd always meant to read? Or perhaps to writing a bunch of crotchety public opinion pieces?

As it turns out, my first job as my own boss was a self-directed assignment. I realized I had to begin writing down some of my untold stories while details and memories remain fresh.

I had a lot to write about. I have lived through some of the nation's most momentous times and challenges: four wars, two depressions, vigorous civil rights movements, incredible tech advances and revolutions, men on the moon, and probes into space. I had gone from a Royal typewriter to an Apple MacBook, from dial phones to hand-held devices, from linotypes and hot metal to word processors, electronic news, and tweets.

During my twelve years as a Seattle councilmember, I worked with three Seattle mayors, cooperated (and sometimes not) with a total of twelve council colleagues, seven terrific staff members, and two dozen volunteer interns. I headed four challenging council committees and two committees of the whole: the Waterfront Committee redrawing Seattle's window onto Elliott Bay, and the newly-approved Metropolitan Parks District that will maintain the city's priceless necklace of parkland, 11 percent of the city's land area.

What I have learned during my journey is that nothing comes easily to many of us, especially women, minorities, and this country's newcomers. Too often we have been held to higher standards, double standards (one for men, another for women), dictated by the mainly white male establishment.

During the 2016 presidential election, we heard from her chief opponents, Donald Trump and Bernie Sanders, that Hillary Clinton was "not qualified" to be president. Hard to imagine a candidate who possessed broader credentials—former senator, secretary of state, and tireless crusader for universal health care. It was also difficult to conceive of two men less capable of judging: a billionaire developer who once owned a beauty pageant and a senator who has been peddling the same rhetoric for a generation. Once again, standards change when applied to women.

Hillary Clinton detractors said she wasn't "likable," one more of those mutable standards. Likability might figure into a voter's choices, but it seems wrong to award the nation's highest office based on "who's better to share a beer with." Rather than pick a president for "likability" or what a candidate "does for fun," I would prefer selecting the leader of the free world for intelligence, resilience, diligence, and experience.

Back in the supposedly liberated 1970s, we foolishly believed women and minorities were at last poised to shatter the glass ceiling, break through an invisible barrier. Then came the backlash. Discomfited males derided feminism. They made dumb blond jokes and defended the old boys club. We discovered that they (the white male leadership) had raised the ceiling to almost unreachable heights.

When someone like Justice Ruth Bader Ginsburg, one of the brightest lights on the Supreme Court, dared speak the truth about Donald Trump, the insult king derided her as "dumb." That is an absurd epithet applied to a woman who authored some of the Supreme Court's most brilliant decisions. Trump tweeted, "Mind is blown; retire." Once again, the old double standard: Men who reach past three-score-and-ten (Trump's age) are assumed to be "mature" and "wise." Women are dismissed as demented.

Even today when a woman speaks out, we hear that she is "shrill," her voice not as deep as the average man's. If she projects her voice so that she can be heard more clearly, she is said to be "shouting." What counts as steely determination and resolve in a man becomes "bitchy" in a woman.

Speaking of the "B" word, I should explain that, during my terms in office, I often was at odds with the *Stranger*, an alternative weekly and blog. The *Stranger* allows its reporters an unusual amount of advocacy and personal bias. Women, especially older women, even those with a liberal outlook, suffer derisive putdowns. But what you can't counter, you can adopt. So when the *Stranger* called me "a bad-ass bitch," I considered it something of a compliment and I often wear a "bad-ass bitch" T-shirt to aerobics classes.

I can recall dozens of other double-standard moments from my own experience, both as a journalist and as a politician. Take the time in 1975 when my boss died unexpectedly and I applied to become the *P-I's* editorial page editor. Publisher Bob Thompson and Executive Editor Jack Doughty granted me the courtesy of a formal interview.

When I left Doughty's office, he said that, on the good side, I had been a serious candidate and I possessed "good legs for an editorial writer." He also said that he liked my "perky walk." These seemed less than relevant qualifications for someone who would be writing about public policy.

Needless to say, I didn't land the editorial page editor job. But I did receive a runner-up award and was appointed "assistant editorial page editor." It was better than nothing, but in a three-person department, it didn't carry a lot of weight.

Five years later, my boss once again departed (this time for a better-paying job) and I became "acting" editorial page editor for the entire next year. Would I be promoted to the full position with better pay? Not likely. After "acting" for a year with a modest six-year reporter's pay, I was told to turn the job over to another man. That man, Charles Dunsire, earned the editorship by writing a series of well-vetted stories about plans to merge the *P-I's* business operations with the *Seattle Times*.

In the aftermath, I was shunted into the *P-I* business editor's job. The position was not sought after because it meant working in tandem with City Editor Tom Sellers. Tom had originally served as business editor and continued to second-guess business page decisions.

As the new business editor, first woman to hold that job, I was met with blatant sexism. Even in the supposedly enlightened 1980s, I heard from executives who asked, "Ms. Godden, what do YOU know about business?" More often than not, press releases and business mail, a sackful each day, came addressed to "Mr. G-e-n-e" Godden.

Yet my 18-month business page tenure had some memorable moments. My four talented reporters and I were badly outnumbered. We competed daily with a dozen business staffers at the rival *Seattle Times*. We managed to stay even with—and sometimes even ahead—of the competition.

An accident of timing helped. We had the dubious honor of reporting on the failure of Seafirst Bank, the state's largest financial institution. Seafirst had invested more than $400 million in "Penn Square," an Oklahoma City bank that dealt in oil and gas industry leases. Then the oil and gas market collapsed. Subsequent losses were staggering. On many days, articles about Seafirst's nail-biting fate became front-page news.

P-I business reporters Bruce Ramsey and Pam Leven ferreted out the unsavory details. They wrote stories about Seafirst's lax loan practices. They wrote about one of the bank's officers who had dressed up like a sheik, drank beer from a cowboy boot, and wore a diamond ring shaped like an oil derrick.

Meanwhile I had created enough discord, demanding independence from the city editor, to be asked to switch jobs. Jim Rennie, the *P-I*'s executive editor, pressed me to write a four-day-a-week city column. He said I could cover anything I wanted except politics, something he reserved for his bearded male columnists.

Writing a city column was a heady assignment since I would essentially be filling a void left when Emmett Watson suddenly quit the *P-I* in 1983. The fabled three-dot columnist (his columns were often made up of short items separated by ellipses)—a man who owned his city—left following an ugly blow-up with Rennie. The executive editor was furious over Watson's negative coverage of Seattle Mariners owner George ("patience is for losers") Argyros. Watson had attacked

Argyros for starving the baseball franchise and constantly threatening to move the team to other cities.

While still smarting from Rennie's expletive-fueled tantrums, Watson was easily lured away. He accepted a better-paying job with The Pacific Institute, a global motivational firm, and began writing his memoirs.

My being handed a city column was eyed with considerable skepticism. Was I being set up to fail? You might think so. But, in my favor, during my days as an editorial writer and business editor, I had acquired many local contacts, countless potential sources. With luck, I managed to learn to swim before I sank.

As a friend of Emmett Watson, I also benefited from a small amount of tutoring. Over lunch before my first column appeared in July 1983 Emmett asked, "What are you planning to write about, kid?" Kid was his nickname for each of his many women friends. (As Emmett himself once said: "I like a strong bench.")

During our lunch, I told Emmett I was distressed about the city cancelling its support for Seattle Rape Relief, a nonprofit assistance program. I said I figured I would write about it. The words were barely out of my mouth when Em put both hands to his forehead and said, "Oh my god! Rape relief."

He told me that, as a columnist, you first have to entertain the troops. Once you have a following, then you can share an opinion. He said, "Let others write about rape relief." He added that what mattered most was to enlighten, enliven, and empower. He shared his mantra: "A column can sometimes be provocative, but never, ever be boring."

Surviving as a columnist was the good news. The bittersweet news came when I learned from union sources that the *P-I* was treating its columnists unevenly. There were five men (some with beards, some who wrote about sports) and me. Can you guess who was paid the least? I did not achieve parity with the guys until 1991 when I left the *P-I* and went to work at the *Seattle Times*.

But, if I thought sexism was rife in the newspaper world, it was because I had yet to experience sexism in the public world. That had to wait a dozen years until I landed on the other side of the reporter's notebook, leaving behind my column-writing career to run for Seattle City Council.

When you aspire to elected office, you quickly realize there are differences between how the media covers male politicians and its treatment of women. There has always been and continues to be vast inequality.

Take for example Theresa May, who became prime minister of Great Britain following that nation's Brexit vote. The media, rather than reporting extensively on her political resume, focused attention on her shoes. According to the British press, the prime minister favors leopard-print shoes with kitten heels. It is hard to imagine similar coverage of a male PM. What did we ever know about former Prime Minister David Cameron's wingtips?

When it comes to media treatment, it isn't only media's preoccupation with appearances, but it is the fact that women's opinions too often go unheard. When appearing with a roomful of candidates, I would often propose an innovative solution, only to have a male opponent echo the exact same approach. Invariably the male candidate would be quoted. There were times when I felt I should cry "plagiarism." But it would only have earned me another "bitchy" label.

Size is another concern for women who dare to run for office. I had always thought of myself as more or less average height (5'3") until I found myself standing at a podium during campaign debates. I realized that audiences were seeing only the top of my head, and that microphones were positioned for a basketball star.

If a group of rival candidates happened to be seated, there were similar problems. Since my height is mostly in my long, bony legs, I sit short and look insignificant, less powerful, like someone's forgotten child.

During my second election campaign, my general election opponent, Green Party candidate Joe Szwaja, was constructed like a barn door. He soon discovered he could make me disappear from sight by standing squarely in front of me. Tired of this tactic (I felt like I was being mooned), I decided to fight back. During a joint appearance at a University District forum, I repeated a story that reporter Lynn Rosellini, Governor Al Rosellini's daughter, once told me.

In 1977, the *New York Times* had assigned Lynn to cover Elvis Presley's funeral in Memphis, Tennessee. She arrived at dawn to stake out a curbside position next to the church. A burly TV camera crew arrived late and set up cameras directly in front of Rosellini, completely blocking the five-foot-tall reporter's view. She asked them to move to one side, please. No dice. She asked again, not so politely. Still no movement. Finally, exasperated, Rosellini took out a ballpoint pen and stuck the point into the cameraman's ribs. He moved.

Perhaps unwisely, I retold Lynn's story and held up my ballpoint pen. Afterwards colleagues accused me of "verbally stabbing" my opponent. I knew I was wrong. But that was the last time Szwaja stood in front of me. Women candidates sometimes have to make the best of a sorry situation.

To be successful, women candidates must project a tough image and avoid any appearance of fragility or ill health. This was especially challenging for me because, try as I might, I had the misfortune to contract some malady during each of my election campaigns.

During my first campaign, I caught a rotten cold that hit 10 days into the campaign. Colds, contracted after so many handshakes, are one of the biggest hazards of campaigning. No amount of hand washing and sanitizing prevents them.

Up at night with a hacking cough, I stubbed my big toe, breaking it. The toe immediately swelled, doubling its size and making it impossible to fit into any of my shoes. I was left to manage throughout half the campaign—the warm weather weeks—wearing a pair of open-toed sandals. Fortunately, the camera focus was seldom on my feet and I learned not to wince when my toe throbbed or when a potential voter bumped into me.

My second campaign was well under way when, to my horror, I discovered blood in my urine. My doctor sent me to the hospital for a kidney scan. There was good news and bad news: My kidneys were clear, but a dark spot on my bladder revealed a tumor that had to be removed.

"Can't it wait until after the campaign?" asked Cathy Allen, my political consultant. No, it could not. But, thanks to creative scheduling, I was able to juggle appearances to allow for a week of surgery and recovery. Better still I managed to escape unwanted press attention.

The third campaign brought an even more challenging health event. I slipped coming downstairs in stocking feet and hit my head, ending with a concussion and a minor stroke. Although barely detectable during an MRI, it was enough to put me in bed for a couple of days, forcing me to miss the annual Gay Rights Parade and a charity breakfast. Fortunately it was not permanently disabling. And, once again, I was able to avoid becoming a news item.

Difficult as it was to run as a woman, it was even more difficult to run as someone past middle age. There is a strong bias against older candidates, particularly older women candidates, more than I could ever have imagined.

It became particularly apparent to me during my third campaign when newspaper articles and blogs started citing my age every single time my name was mentioned. The same outlets neglected to report the ages of less senior candidates.

A lot of ageism, like sexism and racism, is subtle and sneaky, making it harder to correct. If there were stairs to be negotiated, one of my male opponents would thrust out an arm and attempt to help me climb the stairs that I could navigate as well as he. This was especially irritating since, throughout my campaigns, I invariably attracted male opponents. Each subsequent race drew four and sometimes five men, almost all trying to give me a hand.

I knew I was no spring chicken, but I felt that age ought not be a qualification as long as one could be an effective and productive office holder. Ageism is as shabby as sexism or racism. The only way I have found to counter ageism, short of slapping the hand that tries to help me through a doorway, is to make a joke of it.

Humor is an essential, both for one's own frame of mind and for the campaign audiences who appreciate a little levity.

At one candidates' forum, I sat with three male opponents to the left and two to the right. When it came time to introduce myself, I was able to use a joke, saying, "I have jeans older than most of these guys." I also mentioned how ironic that I had to wait until my mature years to become such a guy magnet. "What a shame," I said, "that I never attracted this many guys when I was younger and better looking."

Complaints and challenges aside, I comfort myself that we are finally beginning to do a few things right. More women are actively competing for higher office, running seriously for president, taking leading roles in Congress, the U.S. Supreme Court, in state legislatures and on city and county councils. Seattle has elected a second woman mayor and the Seattle City Council currently has a 6–3 majority of women councilmembers; the Washington Supreme Court also has a 6–3 majority of women justices.

While women officeholders are far from the 50 percent that we are in the general population, we have come a long way. We have had to fight hard for each of our gains, but at last we are shattering glass ceilings. Having watched Hillary Clinton win a major party candidacy for president, having seen her win the popular vote, though—sadly—lose in the Electoral College, we have reached a major watershed. We can assure young women of something young men have long known: There are no limits to their dreams.

Acknowledgments

First, I want to thank the friends I strong-armed into reading early chapters: Mary Lynn Lyke, a travel writer whose editor rated her "one of the best wordsmiths in the business"; Nancy Hevly, a retired *P-I* colleague who edited bestsellers for columnist Emmett Watson and reporter Shelby Scates; and political consultant Cathy Allen, author of four books including *Taking Back Politics*. I am greatly beholden to these women of letters.

I would also like to thank my family members (you know who you are) who put up with me through months of writing and rewriting, but who never second-guessed this project. That's the way to keep family dinners civil.

For illustrations, I am grateful to artist Ramon Collins for his cartoon of Gov. Dixy Lee Ray; to Ruth McCausland for her husband Bob McCausland's cartoon of the freighter that destroyed the West Seattle Bridge; and to SeattleP-I.com/Polaris for permission to use them here. Thanks also to Brad Sherman, Pacific Northwest Newspaper Guild administrative officer, for permission to use strike images, and to Chris Lefebvre for approving use of his dad Dave Lefebvre's cartoon. And finally thanks to the Museum of History and Industry and the Seattle Municipal Archives for use of their images and the *Seattle Times* for permission to reprint my first column.

Many thanks to everyone at Washington State University Press, including my editor Beth DeWeese. The draft I submitted was vastly improved through her patience and professionalism. Beth, along with proofreader Kerry Darnall, kept me from making careless mistakes, "killed my darlings," and gave me confidence the book would someday see print.

I owe gratitude to friends and to several anonymous readers used by WSU Press to assess my draft, make suggestions, and recommend publication (or not). I don't know their names, but their evaluations were astute and their advice invaluable.

Finally, I would like to thank those—far too many to name—who helped me succeed (and sometimes fail) at reporting, editorializing, running for office, serving the city, and trying to make Seattle a better place for all of us. I am grateful to those who voted for me in three general elections. And, perversely, I need to thank those who didn't vote for me when I ran a fourth time. Otherwise I wouldn't have had time to write this book.

If I have missed anyone, please forgive me, allow me to do penance and buy you a cup of coffee.

A Note on Sources

In addition to my own memories, notebooks, and collected newspaper editorials, articles, and columns, I have made use of various sources for this book:

Archival newspapers: Of considerable assistance was the fact that most of the *Seattle Times* is searchable online, through collaboration with the Seattle Public Library. This has been of great assistance when confirming dates. Articles appearing in the *P-I*, most especially my own articles, editorials, and columns from 1974–91 were also of help.

Museum of History and Industry: The archives at MOHAI include numerous excellent pictures.

History Link: Washington is fortunate to have available free online articles focusing on local personalities and important historical events, easily accessed through www.historylink.org.

Seattle City Municipal Archives: The city's archives are an invaluable source of dates, maps, and archived pictures.

Seattle Union Record: Of considerable help was the *Union Record*, published Mondays, Wednesdays, and Fridays by the Pacific Northwest Newspaper Guild, Local 37082, and produced by striking employees of the *Seattle Times* and *Post-Intelligencer*, November 24, 2000, through January 10, 2001.

Additional Sources

Bayley, Christopher T. *Seattle Justice: The Rise and Fall of the Police Payoff System in Seattle.* Seattle: Sasquatch Books, 2015.

Byrd, Joann. "We Don't Do Rumors: But Sometimes, It Might Not Hurt." Edited and produced by Bill Mitchell, Poynter Online. www.poynter.org/news/we-dont-do-rumors-sometimes-it-might-not-hurt.

Campbell, R. M. *Stirring Up Seattle: Allied Arts in the Civic Landscape.* Seattle: Allied Arts Foundation/University of Washington Press, 2014.

Hughes, John C. *Pressing On: Two Family-Owned Newspapers in the 21st Century.* Olympia: Office of the Secretary of State, Legacy Washington, 2015.

Olson, Steve. *Eruption: The Untold Story of Mount St. Helens.* New York: W. W. Norton & Company, 2016.

Scates, Shelby. *War & Politics by Other Means: A Journalist's Memoir.* Seattle: University of Washington Press, 2000.

Stamper, Norm. *Breaking Rank: A Top Cop's Exposé of the Dark Side of American Policing.* New York: Nation Books, 2005.

Stephens, Dave. *Ivar: The Life and Times of Ivar Haglund.* Dunhill Publishing, 1988.

Tunks, Margaret Cary. *Seattle Citizens Against Freeways, 1968–1960: Fighting Fiercely and Winning Sometimes.* Marina Del Rey, CA: M. C. Tunks, 1996.

Watson, Emmett. *Digressions of a Native Son.* Seattle: Pacific Institute, 1982.

Weckworth, Trudy, and Al McVay, eds. *Dixy: Her First Year as Governor of the State of Washington.* Book Publishers Associates, 1977.

Wilma, David W., Walt Crowley, and the History Link Staff. *Power for the People: A History of Seattle City Light.* Seattle: History Ink, 2010.

Index